GOD,

the

GOLD

and the

GLORY

GOD,
the
GOLD
and the
GLORY

Glorifying God Through Personal Increase

BY

LARRY HUTTON

Harrison House
Tulsa, Oklahoma

God, the Gold and the Glory
Glorifying God Through Personal Increase
ISBN 1-57794-131-4
Copyright © 1999 by Larry Hutton
P. O. Box 822
Broken Arrow, Oklahoma 74013

Contents

INTRODUCTION

*F*or many years the subjects of money and material possessions have been very controversial in the body of Christ. People have argued about whether God's children can have substantial amounts of money in their lives and still serve God with their whole hearts. It has been taught and preached that God wants a few people blessed with financial wealth but that the rest of us are to wait until we get to the sweet by and by. Some have gone so far as to say that we should take vows of poverty to deepen our walks with God. Others have said, "Well, it's okay to have your needs met, but God doesn't want you to have too much, or you'll get your eyes off of Him."

When it comes to money, people have many different ideas and numerous questions about how much you can have, what you need and don't need and what you should do with it. Unanswered questions, as well as Scriptures that seem to contradict one another, have left Christians misguided and confused. The Lord told me something about that one time that I believe will help you.

Act on What You Know
✦ ✦ ✦

The first statement He made is something that most of us already know, yet our failure to apply it has hindered our faith. He said, "My Word never contradicts itself. If you think a Scripture is contradicting another Scripture,

7

then it simply means that you are not rightly dividing My Word." (2 Tim. 2:15.)

The second statement He made was this: "Always focus your attention on Scriptures that you know. This will cause your faith to work. Focusing your attention on Scriptures that you don't understand will shut your faith off because when you don't understand a Scripture, the devil can use it to bring doubt and confusion."

And the third statement He went on to make was to tell me to put any Scriptures I didn't understand on the shelf and to ask Him for wisdom concerning them. Then, in time, as I continued to act on and be faithful with the Word that I already knew, more revelation would come and my questions would be answered.

Concerning Healing

✦ ✦ ✦

Let me illustrate, using myself as an example. Many years ago I was sick in my body. Before I received healing in my body from the power of God, I had a lot of unanswered questions concerning the subject of healing. I had questions like these: "If it is God's will for everybody to be healed, then why isn't everybody healed? What about Job's boils? What about Paul's thorn? Is God using this sickness to teach me, humble me or get my attention? Is this my cross to bear? Am I not being healed because I'm special? Was the blindness of the man in John 9 a work of God? When sickness killed Lazarus, was God using it for His glory? Is this what it means to suffer for Jesus?" I could go on and on, but this gives you an idea of some of the questions that I had at the time.

Then after sitting in a good church for a while and hearing that it was God's will to heal all, I began to focus on the Scriptures that I understood. I saw that Jesus never made anyone sick. He never told anyone that healing wasn't God's will for him or her. He never allowed sickness to come on anyone for any purpose. He never told a sick person to suffer for Him. He never told anyone that it wasn't his or her time to be healed. And every sick person that came to Jesus believing he or she would be healed went away healed.

I also saw that Jesus only said what He heard His Father say and did only what He saw His Father do. I realized that Jesus and God are the same today as they were back then, so I exercised my faith on the Scriptures that I understood, and I was healed in my body. Then, as time went by and I kept acting on the Scriptures that I knew, more revelation came and answered the questions I had put on the shelf.

Concerning Finances
✦ ✦ ✦

I have applied the same principle in every other area of the Bible, and I want to encourage you to do the same, especially when it comes to financial prosperity. Since that is the primary subject of this book, then focus your attention on the Scriptures we share. As you read them, begin believing and acting like they're true, because they are!

The Scriptures that I will be sharing with you are ones that our heavenly Father used to teach me about the financial realm. They are easy to understand and will bring faith to your heart if you will zero in on them and begin to act on them. Read over them, meditate on them and start to incorporate them into your daily life. And when you do, Jesus promises in John 8:32 that **ye shall know the truth, and the truth shall make you free.** The more you are filled with God's Word—the truth—the more your revelation knowledge will increase, helping you to better understand God's Word in this area.

So, get started and let God reveal to you the truth that He has established in His Word about this extremely important subject: *God, the Gold and the Glory!*

Part I

GOD

◆ ◆ ◆

✦ ✦ ✦

CHAPTER 1

THE OWNER OF ALL WEALTH·

*F*or too long Christians have bought into the idea that satan owns all of the world's wealth and that riches are evil. Then they reason that it is more spiritual to be poor than to be rich. As a result, many Christians have never really been able to reach their full potential or to fulfill the plan that God has for their lives.

But, as I have studied the Scriptures, I have found quite the opposite to be true. As a matter of fact, I have found that the One who created all of the wealth and called it good is the same One who owns it all today and wants us, as believers, to have it and use it for His glory.

God Called It Good

✦ ✦ ✦

In the beginning, we see God creating the earth and everything in it. (Gen. 1.) Then, in the very next chapter, God tells us,

> **And a river went out of Eden to water the garden; and from thence it was parted, and became**

into four heads. The name of the first is Pison: that is it which compasseth the whole land of Havilah, where there is gold; And the gold of that land is good.

—GENESIS 2:10-12

Since there was gold in the land, as well as other precious jewels, they had to have been created by our Father God during the Creation. Furthermore, verse 12 tells us that gold is *good!* And if you are still in doubt, just look at what God said after He had created everything: **And God saw every thing that he had made, and, behold, it was very good** (Gen. 1:31).

But Genesis isn't the only book in the Bible that speaks of God as the Creator and owner of all the wealth. This truth can be found throughout the whole Bible.

Now therefore, if ye will obey my voice indeed, and keep my covenant, then ye shall be a peculiar treasure unto me above all people: *for all the earth is mine.*

—EXODUS 19:5

Hear, O my people, and I will speak; O Israel, and I will testify against thee: I am God, even thy God.

For every beast of the forest is mine, and the cattle upon a thousand hills. I know all the fowls of the mountains: and the wild beasts of the field are mine. If I were hungry, I would not tell thee: *for the world is mine, and the fulness thereof.*

—PSALM 50:7,10-12

O Lord God of hosts, who is a strong Lord like unto thee? or to thy faithfulness round about thee?

The heavens are thine, the earth also is thine.

—PSALM 89:8,11

O Lord, how manifold are thy works! in wisdom hast thou made them all: *the earth is full of thy riches.*

—PSALM 104:24

The silver is mine, and the gold is mine, saith the Lord of hosts.

—HAGGAI 2:8

For the earth is the Lord's, and the fulness thereof.

—1 CORINTHIANS 10:26

Along with the fact that God is identified as the Creator and the owner of all of the earth's wealth, did you also notice that all of these Scriptures occurred after the fall of Adam and after he gave his dominion to the devil? Does that mean that the devil became the owner of the earth? No! If that were true, how is it then that God was still able to say that the earth and all of its riches belonged to Him?

The God of This Age

✦ ✦ ✦

God could still say that everything belonged to Him because satan isn't the owner of this world. He may be managing it for a while, but he certainly doesn't own it. God does.

Some of the confusion about this comes from a verse in 2 Corinthians 4:4, which calls satan *the god of this world*. But the Greek word, *aion,* which is translated *world* here, actually means "an age, a period of time."[1] The same Greek word is used in Ephesians 2:2 and Romans 12:2, and these verses will help us understand exactly what satan is the god of as we look at them.

> **Wherein in time past ye walked according to the *course* of this world, according to the prince of the power of the air....**
>
> —EPHESIANS 2:2

> **And be not conformed to this *world:* but be ye transformed by the renewing of your mind....**
>
> —ROMANS 12:2

What does it mean that we walked according to the course of this world? That means we were following the prince of the power of the air (satan) and his thoughts and ways. But Romans tells us not to conform to the world's system of thoughts.

By interpreting 2 Corinthians 4:4 in light of these Scriptures as well as the Greek language, we could say that for an age, or set period of time, satan is the god of the ways of this world and has a system, or course, set up for people to follow.

My point in all of this is that satan does not *own* the earth or its possessions; he simply has kingdoms in the earth that he rules over. But thank God we've been translated out of his kingdom of darkness into the kingdom of light!

Understanding this will help you to rightly divide another misunderstood Scripture found in Luke 4:5. This is the account of Jesus being tempted by the devil while in the wilderness. Let's look at verses 5-7:

> **And the devil, taking him up into an high mountain, shewed unto him all the kingdoms of the world in a moment of time. And the devil said unto him, All this power will I give thee, and the glory of them: for that is delivered unto me; and to whomsoever I will I give it. If thou therefore wilt worship me, all shall be thine.**

Jesus knew the devil was a liar. (John 8:44.) However, he also knew that what the devil said here was fact. That had to be the case, or it wouldn't have been a valid temptation. Now, let's look at what the devil said belonged to him.

Notice the devil showed Jesus all the kingdoms of the world. The word *kingdom* also means "rule."[2] We have already found out that satan is the god of this age. Now this verse shows us that he has kingdoms set up to rule during that period of time.

Then the devil said that he would give Jesus the power and glory of them. The word for *power* here means "authority, jurisdiction."[3] And the word for *glory* means "dignity, honour, praise and worship."[4] What the devil was doing was offering Jesus authority, or jurisdiction, over his kingdoms so that Jesus would have the praise and worship of them.

Then the devil said that all of it had been delivered to him and that he could give it to whomever he wanted. The word *delivered* means to "surrender, yield up, intrust, transmit." It also means to "betray."[5] And that is exactly what Adam did in the Garden of Eden. He surrendered, or yielded up, his rule of the earth. He betrayed God and gave satan the authority and jurisdiction over this world.

But, thank God for Jesus, because through His death, burial and resurrection, He defeated the devil and gave back to us all of the authority that Adam had originally walked in. Now we can, according to Romans 5:17, ...**reign in life by one, Jesus Christ.**

A lot more could be said along this line, but our purpose here is to show that satan wasn't telling Jesus that he was giving Him all the wealth of this world. He couldn't do that because he didn't own it. Instead, the devil was trying to get Jesus to see that He could have all of these kingdoms worshipping Him if He would serve him. But Jesus said, **Thou shalt worship the Lord thy God, and him only shalt thou serve** (Luke 4:8).

Notice that Jesus was quoting from Deuteronomy. He was a Master of the law. He knew He was on a mission, and that was to do the will of His Father. Therefore, He carried out the law perfectly. He knew that satan's offer would be of no benefit to Him, so He continued to say only what He heard His Father say and do what He saw His Father do. Jesus was sent to redeem us from the curse that came upon mankind as the result of Adam's transgression. He stuck to it, knowing that His Father would be glorified through His obedience; and thus He fulfilled the great plan of redemption.

The True Giver

✦ ✦ ✦

Now, let's refer back to all of the verses at the beginning of this chapter. We can see clearly that the earth and all of its riches, including the gold, silver, diamonds and all of the other precious gems, as well as the land itself, belong to God. God, not satan, owns the wealth in the earth!

That is why God could say to Joshua, **Every place that the sole of your foot shall tread upon, that have I given unto you** (Josh. 1:3). God could say that because the land belonged to Him. You can't give away something that doesn't belong to you. As a matter of fact, God said the same thing to the children of Israel about the Promised Land. He told them to go search the land that He had given to them. (Num. 13:2.)

God wants you and I to have financial and material blessings as well! And He is willing and able to bless us with them because the earth and all of its riches are His!

CHAPTER   2

✦ ✦ ✦

OUR GOD IS EXTRAVAGANT

God told me one time, "You can't separate riches from My glory." Think about it! Everything that God has created has wealth associated with it! And He did it for us! God is such a giver. At times, He even seems extravagant in His giving and the use of His riches. But, then again, why shouldn't He be? Didn't He create them, and doesn't He own them? We see displays of God's extravagance in the instructions that He left for His places of worship and in how He blessed King Solomon and other men of God with great wealth.

King Solomon Blessed With Wealth
✦ ✦ ✦

Although there were other men of God, such as Abraham, who were blessed with great wealth, King Solomon was one of the wealthiest. Before we look at the wealth he had, let's take a look at some of the wealth God had him use in building the temple. In 1 Kings 6 we see him beginning to build the house of the Lord, which seems to be larger than adequate, especially in light of that for which it would be used. Then we really see God's extravagance in the materials used to build it and decorate it.

Now, as I begin giving dollar amounts, please note that they are just estimates. I looked at numerous references, which included Bible commentaries and Bible dictionaries, and many of them vary from one to the other. However, even though they are estimates, you will get the idea of how elaborate God is as an architect!

Solomon's father, David, had accumulated great wealth for the building of the temple before his death. First Chronicles 22:14 says that he had put aside nearly 3 billion dollars worth of gold! And the weight of the silver was ten times more than that of the gold! We also see in chapter 29, verses 3-4, that David gave out of his own personal wealth an estimated 88 million dollars worth of gold! In addition, we read that David's leaders, the chief of the fathers, the princes and the rulers, gave offerings totaling over 300 million dollars! (vv. 6,7.)

The number of people involved in the building project was mind boggling! Besides the tens of thousands of Solomon's workers, 2 Chronicles 2:17-18 reveals that 153,600 of King Hiram's men from Tyre were sent to carry loads and cut and prepare stones from the mountains.

First Kings 6:21-22 tells us that the whole house, inside and out, was overlaid with pure gold. In addition, verse 32 says that all of the beautiful and cunning carvings of cherubims, palm trees and flowers were also overlaid with gold.

Built of stone and paneled over with cedar, with the whole overlaid with gold, the temple was a work of exquisite taste, stunning beauty and architectural magnificence! It was heavenly! What a display of God's extravagance!

Seven years and six months later, while dedicating the temple that he had finished, Solomon sacrificed offerings unto the Lord using 22,000 oxen and 120,000 sheep. That alone was worth millions! But watch what happens next.

In the following year, he was blessed with still more wealth from the various leaders of the day. The queen of Sheba alone gave him 120 talents of gold, which was again worth millions. He made a throne out of pure ivory and overlaid it with gold; he had a footstool made of pure gold; and all of his drinking vessels were made of gold. According to 2 Chronicles 9:13, Solomon's wages in **gold** for one year were over 19 million dollars! And verse 14 says that that didn't include the gold and silver that came to him from leaders of other countries! Wow! When you read about this, it is hard for the natural mind to comprehend!

Eventually Solomon even built a house for himself, but that's another story in itself. It took him thirteen years to finish it, almost twice as much time as the building of the temple. Can you imagine how nice it was? Then 2 Chronicles 9:25 says that Solomon had 4,000 stalls for horses and chariots and 12,000 horsemen. Second Chronicles 1:15 indicates that in Jerusalem, silver and gold became as plentiful as stones! Can there be any doubt that Solomon was truly an excessively wealthy man? And remember, 1 Kings 3:13 tells us that God is the One who gave Solomon all of his riches!

Of course there are those who will argue against having riches, pointing out that Solomon eventually turned away from God. But it must also be pointed out that, according to 1 Kings 11:1-4, the riches didn't turn him away from God, but his 700 wives and princesses and 300 concubines did him in! Nehemiah 13:26 says, **even him** (Solomon) **did outlandish women cause to sin.**

The Instructions for the Tabernacle and the Ark
✦ ✦ ✦

Now, Solomon wasn't the only one who was given a building assignment from God. Before the temple was ever built God had instructed Moses to build an ark and a tabernacle to house it. An overview of His lavish instructions can be found in Exodus, chapters 25-38.

And they shall make an ark.... And thou shalt overlay it with *pure gold*, within and without shalt thou overlay it, and shalt make upon it a *crown of gold* round about. And thou shalt make staves...and *overlay them with gold*.

Thou shalt also make a table.... And thou shalt *overlay it with pure gold*. And thou shalt make the dishes...*of pure gold*.

And thou shalt make a candlestick *of pure gold*.

—EXODUS 25:10,11,13,23,24,29,31

Moreover thou shalt make the tabernacle. And thou shalt *make fifty taches of gold*, and couple the curtains together with the taches.

And thou shalt make boards for the tabernacle. And thou shalt make *forty sockets of silver* under the twenty boards.

And thou shalt *overlay the boards with gold.*

And thou shalt make a vail of blue, and purple, and scarlet, and fine twined linen of cunning work.... And thou shalt hang it upon four pillars...*overlaid with gold: their hooks shall be of gold,* upon the four sockets of *silver.*

And thou shalt make...the door of the tent.... And thou shalt make for the hanging five pillars... and *overlay them with gold, and their hooks shall be of gold:* and thou shalt cast five sockets of brass [bronze] for them.

—EXODUS 26:1,6,15,19,29,31,32,36,37

I could go on and on and on because this description of the tabernacle continues on through chapter 38! You ought to read it all. It is incredible. We think some of our buildings are beautiful today, but, in comparison, they are just average. Where we use mirrors, pictures, flowers and vases to decorate the doors, walls and floors, they used gold, diamonds, rubies, emeralds and sapphires! Just the decorations alone were probably worth millions!

Can you imagine if we had churches and ministry buildings like the tabernacle of Moses and the temple of Solomon today? We would be attacked from every side! Christians and sinners alike would be stirring up strife, contention, backbiting and envying, saying things like "Those hyperprosperity preachers are just in it for the money."

Yet, it is these same people who, all the while, like to live in nice homes, drive nice cars, wear nice clothes and eat good food. They usually don't turn down raises, promotions or gifts from people. And if any of them have received a large inheritance, I haven't heard a one of them say, "Oh, this is terrible. What a curse this is."

Listen, even though there has been some error concerning the subject of riches in days gone by, and I'm sure there will be more in the days ahead, don't let the error keep you away from the truth of God's Word. Remember, if truth did not exist, there could never be error. Error is merely a perversion of truth. And the truth is that our places of worship, as well as our lives, should bring honor and glory to God, not shame and embarrassment to His people.

The Priestly Garments
✦ ✦ ✦

We can see that God not only wants His *places* of worship to bring Him glory, but He wants *those who worship Him* to glorify Him as well. Notice how specific He was about what He wanted His ministers to wear. Look at Exodus 28. I'm just going to pick out a few verses in this chapter, but if you will read the whole chapter, then you will really get the impact of how particular God was.

And thou shalt make *holy garments* for Aaron thy brother for *glory* and for *beauty*. And thou shalt speak unto all that are wise hearted, whom I have filled with the spirit of wisdom, that they may make Aaron's garments to consecrate him, that he may minister unto me in the *priest's office*.

And they shall make the ephod of *gold*, of blue, and of purple, of scarlet and *fine twined linen*, with *cunning work*.

And thou shalt set in it settings of stones, even *four rows of stones:* the first row shall be a *sardius,* a *topaz,* and a *carbuncle:* this shall be the first row. And the second row shall be an *emerald,* a *sapphire,* and a *diamond.* And the third row a *ligure,* an *agate,* and an *amethyst.* And the fourth row a *beryl,* and an *onyx,* and a *jasper:* they shall be *set in gold* in their inclosings.

—EXODUS 28:2,3,6,17-20

From the above Scriptures it appears that God has nothing against using riches to adorn apparel. After all, it was His idea, not theirs! Just think about the cost of those garments, especially since they were decorated with such precious gems. Clothing like this would cost tens of thousands of dollars by today's standards.

Can you just imagine what would happen if a preacher dressed like that today? The media would be all over him like fleas on a dog! And unfortunately, many immature Christians would be too. But when we look at the Scriptures, it is certainly evident that God has no problem with it.

God wants us to become aware of the truth that He is an extravagant God and that He is delighted and pleased when His children prosper. He is the Creator of all the wealth, and He is more than willing to share it with us when we use it for His honor and glory.

✦ ✦ ✦

JESUS WAS RICH!

*Y*ou may think that the wealthiest man who ever lived was Adam, Abraham or King Solomon, or you may attribute that distinction to an oil tycoon in the Middle East or a computer whiz in the Western world. But I have reason to believe that Jesus had to be the wealthiest man who has ever walked the face of this earth. Now there may be those who think my belief is ridiculous, but let's take a moment and examine it in light of God's Word.

If God is truly the source of all wealth, as we have established, then He knows where all of the gold and the silver are because He created the earth. Jesus said in John 10:30, **I and my Father are one.** Then in John 16:15 He said, **All things that the Father hath are mine.** He knew that meant He didn't have to store up large amounts of wealth to live on because His riches were distributed all over the earth and were at His disposal any time He needed them. If He had wanted to say that His riches were in a bank, He probably would have called it "The First Earth Bank & Trust"!

God, the Father, knew the needs and desires of Jesus and saw to it that His Son's needs and desires were met on a daily basis. The Son had only to trust His Father to lead Him by His Spirit as to where He should go and what He should do. As long as the Son followed through on what the Father told Him to do or to say, He could be secure in the fact that God would provide for all of His needs and desires.

As the perfect example of a man, Jesus was obedient to act on all that the Spirit directed Him to do. And because He had no sin to twist His motives or to hinder Him from hearing what the Spirit would say, He acted in total confidence on the authority that was originally given to Him as a man: to have and exercise dominion over all of the earth.

Let's take a look at a few Scriptures to further establish that the earth and everything in it belonged to Him and that He exercised His authority over its elements and its possessions.

Stilling the Storm

✦ ✦ ✦

Look first of all at Mark 4:35-41, the account of Jesus and His disciples taking a boat across the sea to the country of the Gadarenes. While on the water, a storm suddenly arose. The sea began to swell with huge waves, and the winds were fierce. The ship was being beaten upon by the wind and waves and was filling up with water.

Jesus, awakened by His disciples, spoke to the wind and the sea, and the wind stopped and the waves calmed down. Then, look at the question posed by His disciples in verse 41: **What manner of man is this, that even the** wind and the sea obey him? Jesus exercised His authority over the elements as the Spirit of God led Him.

Blessing Peter

✦ ✦ ✦

But His authority wasn't confined to just the elements. It also included the blessing of man's jobs and businesses. Read, for example, Luke 5:1-7. This is the time that Jesus had borrowed Peter's ship to teach from. After Peter had sown the use of his ship into Jesus' ministry, Jesus told Peter to get back in his ship and let down his nets for a haul of fish.[1] (Luke 5:4.) When Peter acted on what Jesus had said, verses 6 and 7 say,

> **They inclosed a great multitude of fishes: and their net brake. And they beckoned unto their partners, which were in the other ship, that they should come and help them. And they came, and filled both the ships, so that they began to sink.**

Taking into account that fishing was Peter's business and that this was his primary way of providing a living for his family, what happened here was a tremendous financial blessing. Peter's action of sowing to promote the Gospel precipitated Jesus' response to bless Him. Jesus was demonstrating that sowing seed into God's kingdom would always produce a harvest, even when the natural circumstances were pointing to lack. After all, Peter had fished all night and caught nothing! Yet Jesus, demonstrating His authority over circumstances, proved that doing only what He saw His Father do and saying what He heard His Father say would make all of the blessings of heaven accessible!

The Scripture here is showing us that God, the Father, is our source of financial blessings. If we look to our jobs as our source then we, too, may toil all night and come up empty-handed!

Feeding the Five Thousand

✦ ✦ ✦

Another example of Jesus exercising His authority in the area of provision, and evidence that He knew His Father's abundance was available to Him, is found in John 6:1-13. This is the time that Jesus took five loaves of bread and two small fish, which had been given to Him by a little boy, and multiplied them until they were able to feed 5,000 men. (Matt. 14:21.) This number could have easily been 15,000 people or more counting the women and children! That is a lot of people! I don't know if you have ever tried to feed that many people, but think of the money it would take to buy enough fish and bread to feed everyone until they were full and have plenty left over! **And they did all eat, and were filled: and they took up of the fragments that remained twelve baskets full.** (Matt. 14:20.)

Jesus was able to walk in faith in the financial arena because He was led by the Spirit and kept His trust in His Father as provider. This resulted in bountiful blessings to Him, His disciples and all the people that followed Him!

Riding an Untamed Donkey
✦ ✦ ✦

On another occasion, when Jesus was getting ready to make His triumphal entry into Jerusalem, He told two of His disciples to go get His "vehicle" for Him. Look at what He said in Mark 11:2-3:

> Go your way into the village over against you: and as soon as ye be entered into it, ye shall find a colt tied, whereon never man sat; loose him, and bring him. And if any man say unto you, Why do ye this? say ye that the Lord hath need of him; and straightway he will send him hither.

Notice that Jesus wanted this colt, a young donkey, which no man had ever ridden. You might say, "He wanted a brand new vehicle right off the showroom floor!"

Notice also it says the Lord *needed* the colt. Jesus didn't *need* that donkey in the sense that He would be unable to live without it. His use of this donkey to ride into Jerusalem fulfilled Zechariah's prophecy that He who is King of Israel would enter in just this way. (Zech. 9:9.) And remember, Zechariah was speaking the Word of the Lord. This was God's idea! Why didn't God let Jesus walk into Jerusalem? And why ride a donkey? We need to understand that there was nothing degrading about riding a donkey as some have inferred from Zechariah 9:9. Donkeys constituted a considerable portion of wealth in ancient times. (Gen. 12:16; 24:35; 30:43; 1 Chron. 27:25-30; Job 1:3; 42:12.) As a matter of fact, kings, high priests, judges and rich people throughout history have ridden on them.[2] It was His "vehicle," and God wanted Him to ride in style.

Paying His Taxes
✦ ✦ ✦

And what about the account of Jesus sending Peter to catch a fish in order to get money out of its mouth to pay their taxes? It is found in Matthew 17:24-27. Look at what Jesus said in verse 27:

> **Go thou to the sea, and cast an hook** [He didn't tell him to bait it either], **and take up the fish that first cometh up; and when thou hast opened his mouth, thou shalt find a piece of money.**

Who would have ever thought to lower a hook that wasn't baited into the water in order to pay taxes? And notice that Jesus provided for His *and* Peter's taxes. It is obvious from reading verse 24 that *His* taxes were the only ones in question. And furthermore, why didn't Jesus send for Judas, who was the group's treasurer (John 12:6), and have him pay the taxes out of their supply? John 13:29 indicates that Judas must have been called on regularly to take care of their financial matters, so why not this time?

This was another example of Jesus being led by the Spirit and keeping His trust in His Father God. Jesus was demonstrating that we should always look to the Father as our source, regardless of how foolish it may seem to the natural mind, and that we should always be believing God to help meet the needs of others. The result of Jesus' acting on His faith was that His needs and desires were fully provided for.

Jesus Was Ministered To
✦ ✦ ✦

We've seen from all the previous Scriptures that Jesus was a giver! He enjoyed sowing blessings into the lives of others. And from everything we've looked at so far, He was a bountiful giver. Well, God said a bountiful sower would also be a bountiful receiver. (2 Cor. 9:6.) So here's a question to ponder: Do you think that Jesus operated in His Father's law of seedtime and harvest, sowing and reaping, giving and receiving? Yes! He had to receive from His Father to pay His taxes, to bless the fish and bread, to have a donkey to ride into Jerusalem and so on. And further evidence that He received financial and material blessings is found in Luke 8:1-3. This passage says that after Jesus had preached in all the cities and villages, people gave Him love offerings. It says that the twelve disciples, Mary Magdalene, Joanna, Susanna and many others ...**ministered unto him of their substance.** The Greek word for *substance* means "property or possessions."[3] It doesn't tell us here how much property and/or possessions were given Him, but by mentioning the specific ones who gave to Him, as well as *"many* others," then, conservatively speaking, He was substantially blessed with material and financial blessings! The point here is that Jesus not only received financial and material blessings from His Father by exercising His authority upon the earth, but also by exercising the law of seedtime and harvest, thus receiving blessings through the hands of men. (Luke 6:38.) Jesus was indeed rich while He lived on the earth!

What About You?

♦ ♦ ♦

Because Jesus was one with the Father, He really did own all of the gold, silver and cattle upon a thousand hills,

35

making Him the richest man that ever lived on the earth! And because the Father was His source and He was obedient to do all that the Spirit said to do, He had access to whatever He needed or wanted.

We too have access to the Father and all of His blessings just like Jesus did! When we receive Jesus as our Lord and Savior, we become children of God, and as children, we become heirs of God and joint-heirs with Jesus! (Rom. 8:16-17.) Jesus gave us further light in John 17 when He prayed for the children of God: **Neither pray I for these alone, but for them also which shall believe on me through their word: That they all may be one: as thou, Father, art in me, and I in thee, that** *they also may be one in us*...And the glory which thou gavest me I have given them; *that they may be one, even as we are one:* **I in them, and thou in me, that they may be made perfect in one; and that the world may know that thou hast sent me,** *and hast loved them, as thou hast loved me* (vv. 20-23).

Did you know that we are one with God and that God loves us as much as He does Jesus? That is the emphasis of the above verses. Because of Jesus' act of redemption all of our rights and privileges as sons of God have been restored completely. What the first Adam lost by the fall, the second Adam, Jesus, purchased back for us! (1 Cor. 15:45; Rom. 5:17.) And all things that belong to God and Jesus now belong to us! Furthermore, God wants us to have them! *He that spared not his own Son, but delivered him up for us all, how shall he not with him also freely give us all things?* (Rom. 8:32.) Notice God delivered Jesus up for us! Why? So that He could freely give us *all things!* Glory! No wonder God could say that His divine power has already given us all things that pertain to our lives and godliness. (2 Pet. 1:3.)

As we learn to follow the leading of the Holy Spirit and walk in our rights and privileges as children of God, we will enjoy all that God's creation affords. John 15:7 puts it best: *If ye abide in me and my words abide in you, ye shall ask what ye will, and it shall be done unto you.*

✦ ✦ ✦

WHEN DID JESUS BECOME POOR?

*I*f Jesus was the wealthiest man who ever walked on the face of the earth, then why does the Bible say that He became poor for our sakes? Let's take a closer look at that passage and see what it really says. It is found in 2 Corinthians 8:9.

> **For ye know the grace of our Lord Jesus Christ, that, though he was rich, yet for your sakes he became poor,** *that ye through his poverty might be rich.*

A Closer Look

✦ ✦ ✦

Paul, in this chapter, is talking to the Corinthian church about giving to the saints in other churches. He begins by bragging about the generosity of the churches in Macedonia who gave sacrificial offerings to the church in Jerusalem, giving even more than they could afford to give. (2 Cor. 8:1-3; Rom. 15:26.) And then he tells the Corinthians that they, too, need to operate in this same kind of grace. (2 Cor. 8:6.) In fact, Paul praised them for excelling in other areas and then instructed them to excel in the grace of giving as well. Look at verse 7: **But just as you excel in everything—in faith, in speech, in knowledge, in complete earnestness and in your love for us— see that you also excel in this grace kind of giving** (NIV).

Then Paul's boasting turns toward the Lord Jesus when he says, *For ye know the grace of our Lord Jesus Christ...* (v. 9). The Greek word used here for *grace* is the same word Paul used in verse 4, translated "gift," when he refers to the financial donations made by the churches of Macedonia. He also used this same word in his first letter to the Corinthian church, translated "liberality," when he instructed them to give financial and material gifts to the saints in Jerusalem. (1 Cor. 16:1-3.) So, when Paul used this word *grace* in 2 Corinthians 8:9, he was reminding them that Jesus abounded in the same kind of grace he was talking to them about in verse 7—the grace of giving.

Now remember, Paul told them to *abound,* or excel, in this grace of giving. The Greek word for *abound* is "perisseuo" and means to superabound (in quantity or quality) and to be in excess.[1] In other words, God wanted them to be generous and give excessively. Then verse 9 tells us that Jesus exercised that same grace. If Jesus superabounded in His giving, then He must have been rich, which is what our verse goes on to reveal: **For ye know the grace of our Lord Jesus Christ, that, though he was rich....** The Greek word used here for *rich* means "wealthy," or "abounding in material resources."[2] It is used when referring to the rich man of Arimathaea (Matt. 27:57), the rich people casting into the treasury (Mark 12:41), the rich man that died and went to hell (Luke 16:19) and the rich young ruler (Luke 18:23). In fact, 25 of the 28 times we see this word used in the New Testament, it refers to material riches.[3] Further-more, since Paul is talking about literal, material finances within the context of the passage, then to say Jesus was rich financially while on the earth would be a correct and accurate interpretation. This truth is further strengthened as we look at the rest of the verse: ...**yet for your sakes he became poor, that ye through his poverty might be rich.** Notice the words *poor* and *poverty.* Both Greek words used here refer to beggary, poverty and the condition of one destitute of riches and abundance.[4] So when it says Jesus became *poor* it means He became poor materially and financially. He had to have been rich financially in order to become poor financially! Yes, friends, Jesus was rich financially; then He became poor financially so that we could attain financial freedom in our lives.

The Context of the Verse

✦ ✦ ✦

Looking at this verse in light of its context has revealed that Jesus was truly financially wealthy. Paul is saying here that Jesus exercised the grace of giving when He was alive on the earth just like he is exhorting the Corinthians to do. Then he says that Jesus was rich financially and materially while He was exercising that grace, meaning that He was rich when He lived here. Additionally, by looking at our Scriptures in the third chapter of this book, we can see the truth that Jesus was rich while He was on the earth! By rightly dividing God's Word, it has become quite evident that Jesus partook of the financial and material riches that God affords all of His children. And why not? Didn't Jesus have just as much right to God's promises as anyone else? God told Joshua that if he would keep the Word of God in his mouth, meditate in it day and night and be a doer of it, then he would prosper and have good success! (Josh. 1:8.) God told the children of Israel that if they would hearken diligently to His voice and obey Him, then He would bless them everywhere they went and in everything they did, including their jobs and businesses, to the point that they would have so much in their storehouses that they wouldn't have to borrow anymore, but would be in a position to be lenders! (Deut. 28:1-13.) It would be ludicrous to think that God would do any less for Jesus than He did for the rest of His children. We can rest assured that Jesus acted upon God's Word fully and received all the temporal blessings, as well as the eternal ones, which God promises to those who trust and obey. **If they obey and serve him, they shall spend their days in prosperity, and their years in pleasures** (Job 36:11). Therefore we know that Jesus lived in financial freedom, as a wealthy man, on the earth.

Yet, for years I heard people use 2 Corinthians 8:9 to establish their idea that Jesus was poor and lived as a pauper when He was on the earth. They theorized that Jesus was poor after leaving heaven and coming to earth, because this verse says that He became poor for us. However, we now know that there is no scriptural foundation for that assumption. That theory simply cannot be substantiated!

Of course, that raises another question. If Jesus was rich while He was here on earth and this verse says He became poor, then *when* did He become poor? When did Jesus give up all those riches that were afforded Him by the grace of God? Well, this particular passage doesn't give us that information, so we'll have to glean wisdom and understanding from other Scriptures.

For Whom Did He Become Poor?

✦ ✦ ✦

But before we look at a few more Scriptures, let's answer one simple question: "For whom did He become poor?" Look again at the verse: **For ye know the grace of our Lord Jesus Christ, that, though he was rich, yet *for your sakes* he became poor....**

To whom was this written? To Christians! This was written to you and me! Jesus became poor *for our sakes.* He became poor for you and me! This, of course, isn't all that He did for us, so let's take a look at some other things Jesus did for us. Doing so will help us to better understand exactly *when* Jesus became poor.

Jesus Took Our Sins

✦ ✦ ✦

First of all, the Scriptures tell us that Jesus became sin for us. Second Corinthians 5:21 says, **For he [God] hath made him [Jesus] to be sin for us, who knew no sin; that we might be made the righteousness of God in him.** Another translation makes it even clearer: **Christ had no sin, but God made him become sin so that in Christ we could become right with God** (NCV). Notice Jesus became sin so that we could become right with God and live free from the lordship of sin. First Peter 2:24 puts it this way: **Who his own self [Jesus]**

43

bare our sins in his own body on the tree, that we, being dead to sins, should live unto righteousness.

Now the question becomes, *"When* did He do it?" Can we unerringly say that Jesus became sin when He left heaven and came to earth, because heaven is a place of perfection and earth a place where sin abounds? Absolutely not! We know that Jesus was perfect in heaven and remained perfect after He was born of a virgin. Well then, was it when He walked upon the earth as a man? Unquestionably not! The Scripture reveals that He was tempted with every temptation that we humans face, yet He never yielded to their call (Heb. 4:15).

So when did Jesus become sin for us? The Scriptures tell us when He did it. According to 1 Peter 2:24, Jesus bore our sins in His body *on the tree.* In other words, Jesus took upon Himself the sins of the world when He hung upon the cross at Calvary! That is when He became sin. And when the sin came upon Him we see Him cry out, **My God, my God, why hast thou forsaken me?** (Matt. 27:46). That is when God **laid upon Him the iniquity of us all.** (Isa. 53:6.)

Jesus Took Our Sickness
✦ ✦ ✦

But not only did Jesus take our sins away, He took our sicknesses as well. Take a look at Matthew 8:17: **That it might be fulfilled which was spoken by Esaias the prophet, saying, Himself [Jesus] took our infirmities, and bare our sicknesses.**

A careful study of this Scripture reveals that Jesus bore our sicknesses just like He bore our sins. But when did He do it? When did Jesus take our sicknesses and diseases upon Himself? Could we accurately say that He became sick when He left heaven and came to earth, comparatively speaking? Clearly not! Mary didn't have a sick baby! Well then, did He become sick when He lived on the earth as a man? That's absurd! Sickness is an offspring of sin, and sin had no place in Him! (John 7:18.)

So when did Jesus take our sicknesses and diseases for us? At the same time that He bore our sins. And when was that? It was at Calvary! Take a look at the rest of 1 Peter 2:24 and see what it says, **Who his own self [Jesus] bare our sins in his own body on the tree...by whose stripes ye were healed.** In other words, not only did Jesus take our sins in His body so that we could be forgiven, but He also bore our sicknesses in His body so that we could be healed.

Jesus Took Your Poverty
✦ ✦ ✦

Now that we've answered the questions of when Jesus became sin and when He bore our sicknesses, let's look again at our original question: When did Jesus become poor for us? Was it when He left heaven and came to earth? No! Was it when He walked on earth as a man? No! Then He must have become poor and taken our poverty upon Himself at the same time He became sin and at the same time He bore our sicknesses. When was that? At Calvary! When Jesus hung on the cross He not only bore our sins and sicknesses, but He also took the curse of poverty upon Himself so that we could be free from its consequences. This truth is further validated in Galatians 3:13. It reads, **Christ hath redeemed us from the curse of the law, being made a curse for us: for it is written, Cursed *is* every one that hangeth on a tree.**

This verse says that Christ has redeemed us! From what did He redeem us? The curse of the law. But what is the curse of the law? The curse of the law is expounded upon in Deuteronomy 27 and 28, which basically say that if we don't hearken diligently to the voice of the Lord and observe to do all of the commandments that He has commanded us to do, then the curses of sin, sickness, poverty and death will come upon us. But this verse says that Christ redeemed us from that curse when He hung upon the tree! Notice it says He was *made* a curse for us on the tree. This is letting us know, among other things, that He was made, or became, poor for us when He hung on the cross at Calvary!

Now let's look again at our verse in 2 Corinthians 8:9: **For ye know the grace of our Lord Jesus Christ, that, though he was rich, yet for your sakes he became poor, that ye through his poverty might be rich.**

Jesus was rich financially while He lived on earth, then He became poor financially while He hung on the cross. But why did He do that? This verse says He did it for our sakes so that we could become rich. Notice the word *rich*. This is the verb form of the same Greek word used in the first part of the verse and means "to be (or become) wealthy" or to "be increased with goods, (be made, wax) rich."[5] In other words, Jesus became poor and took our poverty upon Himself so that we could become financially free! We now have the blood-bought right to walk free from poverty and be financially blessed in our lives! Glory to God!

By taking the curse of poverty for us, Jesus thus proved that it was the Father's will for us to be blessed with financial and material things in abundance! However, that does not mean that it will happen automatically. Did you notice the verse says that we *might* become rich?

Jesus became poor so that we might become rich. Does that mean that everyone who becomes a Christian will automatically become rich? Well, let me ask you a question: Since Jesus bore the sins of the world, does that mean that everyone is automatically saved? No! John 3:16 says that whosoever will believe on Jesus shall be saved. Romans 10:13 says we have to call on Jesus in order to be saved. Let me ask you another question: Since Jesus bore our sicknesses, does that mean that everyone will automatically be healed? No! James 5:15 says it is the prayer of faith that will save, or heal, the sick. (See Mark 5:23-24 and Mark 10:46-52.) Furthermore, Romans 10:13-14 reveals that we have to hear the Word, believe the Word and then act on the Word before we will get results. There's a process that takes place. We have to hear the Good News, believe it and then receive it. And just like the graces of salvation and healing have to be appropriated by faith, so too does the grace of prosperity. We have to do our part to receive this grace just like we have to do our part to receive saving or healing grace. (See Ephesians 2:8.) And if we don't receive by faith what He did for us, then His work was in vain as far as our individual lives are concerned.

Think about it for a moment. If a person rejects right-eousness (being made right with God by the blood of Jesus), then what Jesus did for them becomes meaning-less. As long as they reject Jesus as Lord and Savior, then the redemption that He provided will never benefit them. Their package of eternal life will remain unopened and unused—even though it was already bought and paid for back at Calvary.

Was it God's will for them to receive salvation? Absolutely! First Timothy 2:4 says that it is God's will for all men to be saved. Second Peter 3:9 says that He isn't willing that any should perish, but that all should come to repentance. Likewise if someone rejects the benefit of physical healing that Jesus paid for on the cross, then that package remains unopened as well. Was it God's will for them to receive healing? Definitely! Psalm 103:2-3 reveals that physical healing is a benefit for members of God's family. Isaiah 53:4-5 unveils that healing was part of our redemptive package that was bought and paid for by Jesus at Calvary. Yet, just because something is God's will doesn't mean that it is going to happen automatically. Even though God is ready and willing to do something for us, we have to do our part and respond to His will to see that it comes to pass. God didn't create robots. He created human beings with human wills capable of making deci-sions and responding to His instructions.

So, what am I saying? I am saying that just because Jesus bore our poverty doesn't mean that we will become rich spontaneously. We have to do our part to receive and act upon this grace that He has provided.

Why Did Jesus Become Poor?

✦ ✦ ✦

Jesus was rich while He was on the earth. But He became poor at Calvary for a reason. Why did Jesus become poor? So that we could become rich on the earth like He was while He was here. Remember, we are now ...**heirs of God, and joint-heirs with Christ** (Romans 8:17). Everything that belongs to God and Jesus now belongs to us, too! Jesus made it possible through His obedience unto death. *Jesus died the way He did so we could live the way He did!* In other words, His life was an example of how God wants His children to live.

Jesus lived on the earth in righteousness, then took the curse of sin for us so we could live a life of righteousness. Jesus lived in health on the earth, then took the curse of sickness for us so we could live a life of health. Likewise, Jesus lived as a wealthy man on the earth then took the curse of poverty for us so we could live a life of wealth. What an exchange He made for us!

This is a part of grace that Christians as a whole have known very little about. Look at our text in 2 Corinthians 8:9 again:

> **For ye know the grace of our Lord Jesus Christ, that, though he was rich, yet for your sakes he became poor, that ye through his poverty might be rich.**

In other words, paraphrasing this verse, "God wants us to know about the grace of prosperity, that is, giving and receiving, which Jesus walked in while on the earth. He lived as a wealthy and generous man, demonstrating to us how God wants us to live, but realizing that we aren't perfect like He is, He had to make a way for us to live like He lived. So He went to the cross and took upon Himself the curse of poverty, so that through that act of love we could become wealthy and be increased with material goods."

A Concluding Thought

✦ ✦ ✦

Jesus walked in total union with His Father. He walked free from sin, sickness and poverty while He lived on the earth. Let me ask you a few questions: How much freedom from sin did Jesus experience? Complete freedom from sin! And how much liberty from sickness did He enjoy? Total liberty from sickness! Then how much independence from poverty did He have? Independence in its entirety! In other words, Jesus was as righteous in the spiritual realm as anyone can be, He was as healthy in the physical realm as possible and He was rich in the financial realm beyond comprehension. Jesus walked in perfection in all areas of His life!

Once you as a believer get a revelation of what Christ has already done for you and the example that He lived, you will no longer tolerate the idea of remaining in poverty or lack. Then you will begin to use your faith to follow God's plan for your life and to be obedient to do all that His Spirit directs you to do. And when you do, you, too, will begin receiving the abundant blessings of the Lord in both the financial and material realms.

✦ ✦ ✦

A SECOND LOOK AT
THE TRADITIONS OF MEN

*T*hus far, we have learned from the Word of God that Jesus was a very rich man while He lived on the earth and that He became poor when He hung on the cross at Calvary for you and me.

However, this is still hard for some to believe (even preachers) because of what has been taught by religion and the religious traditions of men in the past. But, if you can keep an open mind, we will take a closer look at some of those traditions and see how they compare with the Scriptures.

Jesus Had No Place To Lay His Head
✦ ✦ ✦

One tradition that I have heard for many years is that Jesus was so poor that He didn't have a place to lay His head. He had no home to go to, and He was just a vagabond and a pauper. He was a homeless Jesus.

Some have attempted to prove this tradition by using a Scripture found in Matthew 8:20, which says, **The foxes**

have holes, and the birds of the air have nests; but the Son of man hath not where to lay his head. However, a careful study of the Bible reveals that Jesus wasn't saying He didn't have a literal place, or home, to lay His head down at and sleep.

If you will take a closer look at the context of the passage, you will find that Jesus was talking to a religious leader who had come to Him and told Him that he would follow Jesus wherever He went. This man had no idea what that commitment would entail. He didn't realize that Jesus was a preacher who was on the road continually and that He didn't often get to lay His head down in the same bed every night like the foxes and the birds did.

So when Jesus said, **The foxes have holes, and the birds of the air have nests; but the Son of man hath not where to lay his head** (Matt. 18:20), He was letting the man know that if he were going to follow Him everywhere, then he wouldn't be spending much time at home and that he had better get used to laying his head down in a different spot every night.

This is something that I can relate to in my own life and ministry. My family and I, as well as other traveling preachers and teachers, are rarely home for any length of time; and we find ourselves laying our heads down in different beds continually as we stay in various accommodations around the world. But that doesn't mean that we don't have a home to go back to where we can rest up between ministry opportunities!

Likewise, just because Jesus emphasized to this religious leader the kind of life he would be signing up for if he decided to follow Him doesn't mean that Jesus didn't have a home to live in as He fulfilled His ministry on the earth. As a matter of fact, the Scriptures reveal that Jesus lived in a home the whole time He was here!

Did Jesus Have a Home?
✦ ✦ ✦

First of all, the Scriptures tell us that He lived in Nazareth with His parents until He was about thirty years old. Then after His famous sermon in the synagogue about His anointing from God to preach, heal and deliver people, the people rose up and threw Him out of the city. (Luke 4:18-29.)

That is when the Bible tells us that He moved to Capernaum. Look at Matthew 4:13: **And leaving Nazareth, he came and dwelt in Capernaum.** Capernaum was located on the coast of the Sea of Galilee. This is the area where Peter, Andrew, James and John lived. Notice our verse says Jesus *dwelt* there. The Greek word used here for *dwelt* means "to house permanently" or "reside."[1] In other words, Jesus was residing, or living, in a house permanently in Capernaum. He wasn't living outside under a tree!

But let's not just consider one Scripture; look at what other Scriptures say as well:

> **And again he entered into Capernaum after some days; and it was noised that he was in the *house*.**
>
> —MARK 2:1

> **And he came to Capernaum: and being in the *house* he asked them....**
>
> —MARK 9:33

The same day went Jesus out of the *house*, and sat by the sea side.

—MATTHEW 13:1

Then Jesus sent the multitude away, and went into the *house:* and his disciples came unto him....

—MATTHEW 13:36

And when he was come into the *house,* his disciples asked him privately....

—MARK 9:28

And when they were come to *Capernaum,* they that received tribute money came to Peter, and said, Doth not your master pay tribute? He saith, Yes. And when he was come into the *house*....

—MATTHEW 17:24,25

After this he went down to *Capernaum* (where He lived), he, and his mother, and his brethren, and his disciples: and they continued (dwelt) there not many days.

—JOHN 2:12

When the people therefore saw that Jesus was not there, neither his disciples, they also took shipping, and came to Capernaum, seeking for Jesus. (Why? Because that's where He lived!)

—JOHN 6:24

There is one more passage of Scripture that I want you to look at before we continue. It is found in Matthew 9. Verse one tells us that Jesus returned from a ministry trip via ship to Capernaum. And verses 2 through 26 reveal a number of other ministry opportunities that Jesus was involved in within the local area. Then when Jesus was returning home, two blind men started following Him. And verse 28 says, **And when he was come into the** *house,* **the blind men came to him.** Then verse 31 tells us that after they were healed, they, not Jesus, departed from the house. The Greek word for *house* refers to a "residence"[2] and is used when referring to Peter's home (Matt. 8:14), Jairus' home (Mark 5:38), the home of Simon the leper (Mark 14:3), the home of Levi the publican (Luke 5:29), the centurion's home (Luke 7:6) and the home of a Pharisee (Luke 7:36).

Now we can readily see that Jesus lived in Capernaum, and, based upon these Scriptures, we know He lived in a house. And we also know that He used this house for other ministry opportunities besides healing the blind men. In fact, Matthew 9:2-7 speaks of a paralyzed man that came to Jesus for healing. Paralleling this passage with its counterpart in Luke 5:19-25, it appears that all of this took place in the house in which Jesus lived. Whether it was a big house is not known for certain, but it was big enough to hold a meeting that included a multitude of Pharisees and doctors of the law who came ...**out of every town of Galilee, and Judaea, and Jerusalem** (Luke 5:17).

"Okay, Brother Larry, I admit Jesus did have a house to live in, but the Scriptures don't specifically state that it was *His* house."

That's true. The writer of each reference did say that Jesus went into *the* house. However, think about who wrote each of the references. Matthew and Mark did, and their relationship with Jesus was a very intimate one.

They were Jesus' ministry staff and just like family to Him. So when they spoke of the house, it would have been likely for them to be referring to Jesus' house.

Let me illustrate. If you came into my town and started talking with people who were close to me—my wife, ministry staff or other family members—and you asked them where I was, they might say something like "He's over at the house" or "He went to the house for a few minutes." If you stopped by my office and talked to my administrator, and he said, "Oh, I wish Brother Larry were here, I know he would love to see you. But he left just a few minutes ago and told me he would be at the house if I needed him," whose house would you think he was referring to? Mine, of course! Now if someone were *reading* his statement, there would be no way to absolutely prove that he was referring to my house, but we know that he was.

Further evidence that Jesus owned His own home is brought to light when we realize that Jesus walked in the full and abundant provision of His Father. God said in Psalm 112:1-3, **Blessed is the man that feareth the Lord,** *that* **delighteth greatly in his commandments...wealth and riches shall be in** *his house*....

Furthermore, when God was telling the children of Israel about the blessings of obedience, He warned them not to forget Him after they received the promised blessings. Look at what God said in Deuteronomy 8:12 NIV: **Otherwise, when you eat and are satisfied, when you build fine houses and settle down....** God promised them that part of the provision of living in the Promised Land would be to build their own nice homes!

In addition, I'll refer to Deuteronomy 28, which speaks of the blessings and the curses of the law. When God was citing the curses, He said, ...**thou shalt build an house, and thou shalt not dwell therein** (v. 30). A study of this chapter reveals that the curses were the opposite of the blessings. Consequently, those who walked in obedience were promised that they could build homes and dwell in them!

Do you believe that God would promise and provide any less for Jesus than He did for the children of Israel? Of course not! We know that Jesus walked in the abundance of God's blessings spiritually, mentally, physically and financially. Then it is relatively easy to believe that if they could have their own homes, so could Jesus!

Furthermore, do you remember that Jesus was a carpenter before He was a preacher? (Mark 6:3.) He had learned the trade from His father, Joseph. (Matt. 13:55.) Well, how good of a carpenter do you think He was? Most Christians would have no difficulty believing that Jesus became one of the best, if not the best, carpenters in the land! We're told in Luke 2:51-52 that while He lived at home with His parents, which is when He practiced carpentry, He increased in wisdom and favor with man. One thing that we can ascertain from this account is that He became highly skilled and had a good reputation as a carpenter.

Well, that would lead one to consider the possibility that Jesus built His own home when He moved to Capernaum. After all, being a carpenter, what would have kept Him from building a house for Himself, as well as a place from which to base His ministry?

So, whether or not Jesus built the house in Capernaum or bought it, taking into consideration all that we've looked at thus far, it was more than likely His home. And since there are no Scriptures that would indicate otherwise, then that would give further credence to this belief.

Search the Scriptures

✦ ✦ ✦

I pray that you have had your eyes opened, like I have, about some of the things that we've heard for many years—things like Jesus being poor, not having a place to lay His head and no home to go to. These traditions of men have blinded Christians' eyes from seeing the light of the glorious Gospel in this area of prosperity. So I challenge you, the reader, not to blindly accept every wind of doctrine that comes blowing through, but to examine what you hear by the Word of God. Develop your skill and ability to rightly divide God's Word, and become like the Berean Christians who received the Word eagerly but also studied what Paul and Silas taught to see if what they were teaching was really so. (Acts 17:11.)

Part II

THE GOLD

◆ ◆ ◆

✦ ✦ ✦

GOD'S WILL FOR YOU

*I*n the previous chapters, we have seen that it is our heavenly Father's will for us to be blessed with financial and material wealth. Jesus paid an awesome price at the Cross just for you and I to have this blessing in our lives. However, the first step in obtaining the financial freedom that God has for us is to be convinced through His Word that it is His will for us to prosper, personally, and not be in lack.

The only way for that to happen is to get more understanding from God's Word in this area. His Word will light up our paths and show us the way to His blessings. The psalmist said, **Thy word is a lamp unto my feet, and a light unto my path** (Psalm 119:105.)

To further establish our minds and hearts in His Word, let's take a look at 3 John 2.

His Will for Believers

✦ ✦ ✦

This is a very candid verse of Scripture. It says, **Beloved, I wish above all things that thou mayest prosper and be in health, even as thy soul prospereth.**

John was writing this to a brother named Gaius. Gaius was baptized under Paul's ministry (1 Cor. 1:14), traveled with Paul (Acts 19:29) and was from the town of Derbe (Acts 20:4). But is it possible that when John wrote this letter to Gaius God inspired him to write it, knowing that it would be for our benefit as well? Does this verse apply to you and me today? Let's take a closer look and see. First of all, the mere fact that this letter was canonized into Scripture indicates that this verse is for us. And even though it was written to an individual, so were letters to Timothy, Titus and Philemon; but we know that they were also written for our benefit. Furthermore, John makes the statement, in verse 4, that there was no joy greater than the joy he received when he heard that God's children were walking in the truth. The fact that he said "my children" is further proof that God intended for you and I to benefit from this passage of Scripture. You and I are just as much the children of God as were the original readers of these letters. And then, finally, 2 Timothy 3:16-17 tells us that all Scripture is God-inspired and given to His children for their benefit so they can live the way He wants them to. So, when John begins this verse by calling Gaius the "Beloved," I know that God is speaking here to you and me as well. John even calls us "the beloved" in the third and fourth chapters of his first epistle.

Then, what is God saying to us, His beloved? He starts out by saying, "I wish." The words *I wish* come across a little stronger in the Greek and could have been translated *I pray* or *I will*.[1] In other words, this is God's prayer for us and His will for us. Now, if something is God's will for us and His prayer for us, then it must be important to Him.

In fact, He says that it is His prayer and will for us *above all things*. That sounds like it's pretty important to me. To say "above all things" would indicate top priority!

Prosper and Be in Health
✦ ✦ ✦

Now what exactly is it that He wills for us? Well, first of all, He mentions two things: that we prosper and be in health. Some would have us believe that this just means spiritually and that God wants you to prosper spiritually and be healthy spiritually.

Actually though, this word *prosper* comes from a Greek word that means "to help on the road" and, in a figurative sense, "to succeed in business affairs" or "to have a prosperous journey."[2] To help on what road? To prosper on what journey? The road of life and its journey! God wants us to prosper and succeed in our business affairs while traveling the road of life. There are only two other Scriptures that use this Greek word in the New Testament. Both refer to following God's plan in life. The first is found in Romans 1:10, where Paul refers to his desire to have a prosperous journey to visit the beloved of God in Rome. The other is found in 1 Corinthians 16:2, where Paul is encouraging the church there to lay aside some finances, as God has prospered them, to give to the Christians in Jerusalem.

This shows that John is not referring to spiritual prosperity here in 3 John 2. He addresses that at the end of the verse when he talks about our souls prospering. And we know he is not referring to our bodies because he talks about that when he says, "be in health." So, with those considerations, it appears that he is referring to the financial and material realm.

As far as the word *health* is concerned, the Greek word means to "be well in body."[3] I don't think there is any way you can spiritualize that definition. This is definitely referring to our physical health, or what I call physical prosperity!

Prospering in Your Spirit
✦ ✦ ✦

However, the rest of this verse reveals an important key that pertains to the financial and physical prosperity that we will experience in this life. It says ...**even as thy soul prospereth.** What does God mean when He says, *even as?* Essentially, He is saying that the prosperity He wants us to have in the financial and physical realms is going to be in direct proportion to the prosperity we have in our souls.

The Greek word used here for *soul* means "the breath of life."[4] It can be found 105 times in the New Testament with various applications[5] and can be interpreted as referring to either the spirit or the soul, depending upon the context. By the mere fact that the Greek word means "breath of life," we know that this word *soul* refers to our spiritual prosperity; in other words, prospering in our hearts. But this word is also translated "soul," meaning the intellectual part of man, which includes the mind, will and emotions. I believe that God is referring to both types of prosperity here; that is, prospering in our hearts and in our heads. Why? Because John says to Gaius in verses 3 and 4 that the brethren testified that the truth was in him and that he was applying it to his daily Christian walk. Now, in order to have the Word in us and then apply it to our everyday lives, we have to be prospering in our spirits and our souls.

How then do we prosper in our spirits and souls? In order to prosper in our spirits, we must first of all be born again. Jesus said, **Ye must be born again** (John 3:7). In the previous verse He calls it being born of the Spirit, and then He tells us in verse 16 that the result will be everlasting life, which He refers to as being saved in the next verse. How do we get saved? Romans 10:9 tells us that if we confess Jesus as our Lord and believe in our hearts that God raised Him from the dead then we will be saved. Confessing as Savior any other man or god does not save us! In the fourth chapter of Acts we see Peter preaching to the Jews about Jesus the Savior. Then in verse 12 he says, **Neither is there salvation in any other: for there is none other name under heaven given among men, whereby we must be saved.** Jesus is the only way to heaven! When we receive Him as Lord and Savior we are reborn in our spirits and become brand new creations in Him.

Second Corinthians 5:17 TLB puts it this way: **When someone becomes a Christian, he becomes a brand new person inside. He is not the same anymore. A new life has begun!** Notice it is the man on the inside, or our spirit man, that becomes new. That is the start of spiritual prosperity in our hearts. But what about our bodies and our souls? Do they become new? No. It is quite easy to see that if someone is bald before receiving Jesus, he or she is still bald after receiving Jesus. If someone is short in stature before receiving Jesus, he or she is still short afterwards.

In other words, our physical bodies don't become new. We will receive new glorified bodies when Jesus comes to take us with Him. (See 1 Corinthians 15:52-53.)

Prospering in Your Soul

✦ ✦ ✦

And what about the soul that contains our thoughts and feelings? Do we automatically have perfect thoughts and feelings once we're saved? No! Again, it is made clear to us that God's ways and thoughts have to be learned. We're told in Romans 12:2 that it is our responsibility to renew our minds to God's thoughts and ways so that we don't conform to the world's ways of doing things.

And be not conformed to this world: but be ye transformed by the renewing of your mind, that ye may prove what is that good, and acceptable, and perfect will of God.

And how do we renew our minds? God tells us in Isaiah 55:8-11 that His Word will produce the fruit of His thoughts and ways in our lives. We have to hear God's Word over and over until we learn it—then we can think His thoughts and walk in His ways. James tells us that when we receive God's Word it will save our souls. (James 1:21.) That is how we prosper our souls. Romans 10:13-14,17 says it this way:

For whosoever shall call upon the name of the Lord shall be saved. How then shall they *call* on him in whom they have not believed? and how shall they *believe* in him of whom they have not heard? and how shall they *hear* without a preacher?

**So then faith cometh by hearing, and hearing
by the word of God.**

Notice the three words that are italicized—call, believe
and hear. This verse tells us that once we hear about Jesus,
we can believe in Him. Once we believe in Jesus, we can
call on Him. And once we call on Jesus, we will receive
from Him whatever it is we are calling on Him for!

Someone may say, "That isn't what it says! It says whosoever calls on Jesus will be saved." Yes, that is true, but don't
you remember that Jesus has saved you from more than just
sin? He has also saved you from sickness and poverty!

When the woman with the issue of blood heard about
Jesus, she went and called on Him, and her faith made her
whole. (Mark 5:25-34.) When Peter saw the lame man at
the gate called Beautiful, he called on the name of the Lord,
and his faith in that name brought the lame man a miracle.
(Acts 3:1-16; 4:22.) When Jesus told Peter to get in his ship
and let down his nets for a catch, Peter acted on His Word,
and he received prosperity! (Luke 5:4-7.) Jesus is more than
just a Savior from sin. The woman called on Him as her
healer. Peter looked to Him as miracle worker for the lame
man and then as provider of material blessings on the other
occasion. Jesus is Jehovah-Rapha, our healer. (Exodus 15:26.)
He is Jehovah-Jireh, our provider. (Gen. 22:14.)

But the point I'm wanting to make here is this: You
can't *call* on Him as your healer if you don't believe He will
heal you. And you can't *believe* He will heal you if you
haven't heard that He will. And you can't *hear* that Jesus
heals if someone doesn't preach that He does!

Likewise, you can't call on Jesus as your provider if you don't believe He wants to provide for you. And you can't believe He wants to provide for you if you don't hear about it. And you can't hear if you don't listen to someone preaching that Jesus wants to provide for you!

Why not? Because **faith cometh by hearing, and hearing by the word of God** (Rom. 10:17). It is impossible to have faith for something if you don't hear the Word of God on the subject. So you must hear before you can really believe.

Now let's go back to our original text in 3 John 2, **Beloved, I wish above all things that thou mayest prosper and be in health, even as thy soul prospereth.** Using all of the definitions that we have already looked at, let me paraphrase this verse for you:

"Dear Child of God, it is My will for you and a top priority prayer of Mine that while you are living on the earth, you would prosper financially and also be healthy in your physical body. This will happen as a direct result of your filling your heart and renewing your mind with My Word on these subjects."

Before we close this chapter on God's will concerning our prosperity, let's look at something David said in the Psalms. Even though David made many mistakes in his life, he had a heart after God, which always brought him back to God. And God prospered David in all areas of his life. First Chronicles 29:28 says that David **died in a good old age, full of days, riches and honour.** Now, with that in mind let's look at something David said in Psalm 35:27. In the latter part of the verse he says, **Let the Lord be magnified, which hath pleasure in the prosperity of his servant.**

Did you hear what David said? He said it brings our Father pleasure when we prosper! That must mean that it is God's will and desire for prosperity to be in our lives. If not, then it surely wouldn't please Him. But thanks be unto God that we have a heavenly Father who wants us to prosper and takes great delight in our prosperity!

However, we have found out that God's desire for us to prosper financially does not mean that prosperity will happen to us with no effort on our part. Once we accept His will for prosperity in our lives, then we have to do our part by hearing, believing and acting upon the Scriptures that deal with prosperity. It is our responsibility to find a good church that teaches this wonderful truth and to get busy filling our hearts with God's Word and renewing our minds. Then we can experience the prosperous life that God has intended for us to have.

✦ ✦ ✦

WHY GOD WANTS US TO PROSPER

*I*f we want God to prosper us as He has said, then we need to have a clear understanding of the reasons God wants us to prosper. Once we truly have an understanding of why God wants us to prosper, then we can receive God's financial blessings without the risk of hindering our walk with Him. We will be able to fulfill the plans and purposes that God has for us and more effectively promote His kingdom.

Based on all that I have studied in this area, I would have to say that there are four main reasons for God's financial blessings in our lives: (1) to let us know that He loves us like a Father, (2) to promote the Gospel, (3) to meet the needs of other Christians and (4) to give to the poor.

Because He Loves Us

✦ ✦ ✦

Yes, it is true. The number one reason God wants us to prosper and be financially free is because He loves us! "But, Brother Larry, I thought the main reason God wants us to have riches is to preach the Gospel."

I thought that too at one time, until God corrected my theology. One day I was in my prayer closet when God asked me a question, "Larry, do you know the main reason I want you to prosper financially?" I said, "Yes, Lord, You want me to prosper so that I can get the Gospel out."

When I waited to hear what He would say, His answer surprised me as He said, "No, that isn't the main reason I want you to prosper. The main reason I want you to prosper is that I love you."

When He said that it brought tears to my eyes, and I said to Him, "Do You mean You want me to have riches just because You love me?"

His response was, "Yes."

Then I said, "Lord, I've never heard that before. You're going to have to show me that in Your Word."

Lovingly, He said, "Larry, in the beginning before there was ever a Gospel to preach, a need to supply or a poor person to give to on the earth, I was your heavenly Father. I created all the wealth not for you to give away, but for you to enjoy and to bring you pleasure."

Then He went on to reveal to me that He is Jehovah-Jireh, the Lord who sees after us and provides for us. (Gen. 22:14.) And when He created all the riches on the earth, it was for the pleasure of His kids, you and me. When He created the wealth on the earth, it was for the sole purpose of man's enjoyment.

Later on, God asked me this question: "Larry, when you give things to Rachel, your daughter, are they for her to give away?"

After thinking about it for a moment, I said, "No, Lord, they aren't. Of course I want her to share and be willing to give of what she has, but my main reason for giving to her is that I love her as a father, and I want her to have things for her enjoyment."

Then He explained to me, saying, "That's what I'm like, except that I'm a how-much-more God, and I can do much more than you can."

And you know, He is right! He can do so much more than you or I ever could. Look at what He says in *The Amplified Bible* in Matthew 7:11:

> **If you then, evil as you are, know how to give good and advantageous gifts to your children, *how much more* will your Father Who is in heaven [perfect as He is] give good and advantageous things to those who keep on asking Him!**

When I was growing up in church, I was always taught that this meant spiritual things, but it doesn't! If you will look at the Scripture within its context and go back to chapter 6, you will find that God isn't referring there to spiritual things, but to natural things. He is talking about not seeking after money, clothing and food, but He tells you rather to seek first His kingdom and promises that all these things will be added to you if you do.

Then in Matthew 7, prior to verse 11, He reasons as follows: "If your children asked for bread or fish, you wouldn't give them something bad, would you? No, of course not! And if your children asked for some bread, you'd probably give them the bread and some peanut butter and jelly too!"

This, of course, is my paraphrase, but the point He is leading up to is that we know how to give good gifts to our children. But He doesn't stop there. He goes on to draw an analogy about Himself, saying, "If you think that you, as an imperfect being, give good gifts to your children, then I want you to know that I'm a God of *how much more,* and I will give *good things* to My children when they ask Me for them!"

When I began to realize what God was saying here, I was overwhelmed by His love. I saw for the first time that the number one reason for any of God's blessings being given to me was that as my Father, He loves me. He wants me saved because He loves me. Yes, He wants me to share that love with others, but the *first* reason is that He loves me! He wants me healed because He loves me. He wants me filled with the Holy Ghost because He loves me. He wants me full of peace and joy because He loves me, and He wants me prosperous *because He loves me!*

But He doesn't love just me. He loves you too! And to receive all that He has for you, you are going to need to be convinced of His love for you and of His desire to bless you. So, let's look at a passage of Scripture that will further substantiate that God's *first* purpose for prospering you is that He loves you and wants you blessed.

Establishing the Covenant
✦ ✦ ✦

In the past, whenever I had preached on Deuteronomy 8:18, I had always used it to point out that the first reason for prosperity was to spread the Gospel. But when

God told me that the number one reason was because He loved me, then I had to reconsider what He was saying in Deuteronomy. So He brought me to this verse and showed me something I hadn't seen before.

> **But thou shalt remember the Lord thy God: for it is he that giveth thee power to get wealth, that he may establish his covenant which he sware unto thy fathers, as it is this day.**
>
> —DEUTERONOMY 8:18

Notice that this verse says God gives us power to get wealth. Well, it must be His will then for us to have wealth! (He wouldn't give us the power to get wealth if He didn't want us to have it. That would be stupid!) Then the verse goes on and tells us the purpose for getting the wealth: ...**that he may establish his covenant which he sware unto thy fathers, as it is this day** (v. 18).

For years I paraphrased this verse, saying, "God gives us power to get wealth so that we can establish His covenant on the earth (preach the Gospel)."

"Well, Brother Larry, isn't that what it says?"

My answer to that question is "That is part of what it is saying, but not all of what it is saying." Let me explain. Notice that verse 18 doesn't say, "establish His covenant on the earth." It says, ...**establish his covenant which he sware unto thy fathers**.... In other words, there was a covenant that God made with our fathers—Abraham, Isaac and Jacob—that He wants to establish in our lives.

According to this verse, using the power that He gives us to gain wealth has something to do the covenant

75

He made with our fathers. Let's go back to Genesis chapters 12 through 15 and find out what that covenant was.

I Will Bless You

✦ ✦ ✦

If you read these chapters, you will see that God's covenant included the acquisition of great wealth—financially and materially. Space doesn't permit me to quote all of the verses, but I will point out a few key ones. Let's begin with Genesis 12:1-3:

> **Now the Lord had said unto Abram, Get thee out of thy country, and from thy kindred, and from thy father's house, unto a land that I will shew thee: And I will make of thee a great nation, and I will bless thee, and make thy name great; and thou shalt be a blessing: And I will bless them that bless thee, and curse him that curseth thee: and in thee shall all families of the earth be blessed.**

God told Abraham that it was time to move to a new land; then look at what He said to Abraham in verses 2-3: **...and I will bless thee, and make thy name great; and thou shalt be a blessing...and in thee shall all families of the earth be blessed.**

Notice that when God started talking about blessings, He told Abraham, "I'm going to bless you first." Now, some would have you believe that God just meant spiritual blessings, but notice Genesis 13:2: **And Abram was very rich in cattle, in silver, and in gold.** Don't try to spiritualize this verse. God wasn't talking about spiritual

76

"moo-moos"! Neither was He talking about spiritual silver or gold! No, He was talking about riches. As a matter of fact, the sixth verse of that chapter reveals that Abraham and his nephew Lot could not dwell in the same land together because their substance was too great! Abraham walked in the realm of too much!

But just in case you don't believe God was the One who made him rich, look at Genesis 24 where Abraham had sent his servant to find Isaac a wife. After meeting Rebekah and her family, listen to what the servant said.

> **I am Abraham's servant. And the Lord hath blessed my master greatly; and he is become great: and he hath given him flocks, and herds, and silver, and gold, and menservants, and maidservants, and camels, and asses.**
>
> —GENESIS 24:34,35

This servant didn't just say, "The Lord blessed my master." He said that God had blessed Abraham *greatly!* And the blessings from the Lord that he was referring to were riches and material possessions in abundance.

So, here in Genesis 12:2, God was including riches and material possessions when He told Abraham, ...**I will bless thee, and make thy name great; and thou shalt be a blessing.**

You Will Be a Blessing

✦ ✦ ✦

The second thing that God told Abraham was "You shall be a blessing." In other words, God was letting Abraham know that after he was blessed, then He expected him to turn around and be a blessing to others. This covenant of being blessed and being a blessing to others wasn't just for Abraham. As a matter of fact, it was for all families of the earth because He goes on to say ...**and in thee shall all families of the earth be blessed** (v. 3).

Did you see your family name in that verse? It is there! If you are the seed of Abraham, then you are one of the families this verse is talking about. Look at what Galatians 3:16,29 says about Abraham's seed: **Now to Abraham and his seed were the promises made.... And if ye be Christ's, then are ye Abraham's seed, and heirs according to the promise.**

God's covenant with Abraham was to first bless him, then to bless others through him, and finally it was to establish this blessed covenant in the lives of the seed of Abraham. We need to see here that God was telling Abraham that He wanted to bless him first. Why? Because God is love. His covenant was a covenant of love, so He was blessing Abraham because He loved him.

Now let's go back to Deuteronomy 8:18:

But thou shalt remember the Lord thy God: for it is he that giveth thee power to get wealth, that he may establish his covenant which he sware unto thy fathers, as it is this day.

Notice here that God gives us power to get wealth so that He can establish His covenant with us as He established it with our father Abraham. That means that God wants to bless us first because He loves us! He wants us to have riches and possessions in abundance because He created them for us to enjoy. He wants us to possess enough riches so that we will require no aid or support and so that we will become lenders rather than borrowers. That is the first part of God's covenant with us.

Then, not only does He love us, but He wants us to bless others so that He can establish this blessed covenant in their lives as well. I can't think of a better way to be a blessing to others than using the wealth God gives us to spread the Gospel! Establishing His covenant in the lives of others is what spreading the Gospel is all about. We're supposed to be blessed to be a blessing!

Look at 2 Corinthians 9:8 from *The Amplified Bible:*

And God is able to make all grace (every favor and earthly blessing) come to you in abundance, so that you may always and under all circumstances and whatever the need be self-sufficient [possessing enough to require no aid or support and furnished in abundance for every good work and charitable donation].

This Scripture reiterates the first two reasons that God wants us to prosper. Let's take a closer look. Notice the verse says that God will make His grace come to us in abundance. This is the same grace that Jesus demonstrated in 2 Corinthians 8:9, which we studied about in our third chapter. Since Jesus bore our poverty for us, we too can exercise this same grace. And when we do, then God makes His grace abound to us. He causes favor and earthly blessing to come to us in abundance. Why? So that we can always have more than enough no matter what need or circumstance we are facing and have plenty left over to give to ministries and organizations that are promoting the Gospel.

Think about it for a moment. How many good works do you know about? You probably know a considerable number of them. And this verse says that God wants us to abound, or give in excess, to every one of them. In other words, He wants us to be able to give them *more* than they need. But in order to do that, we will have to be operating in abundance. And that is exactly God's point. He wants us to be totally financially free so that we can give generously and thus fulfill the second half of the covenant: to be a blessing to others.

Besides that, when we have a heart after God, we won't want to hoard everything up for ourselves. We will be givers just as God is a giver! God didn't hoard all of the riches up in heaven for Himself. Instead, He gave us a whole bunch of them down here for us to enjoy. However, wealth and riches aren't the issue here; rather, the issue is the establishing of His covenant in the lives of others by spreading the Gospel. The majority of our enjoyment of being wealthy is in being a blessing to others. This is the second reason that He wants us to prosper.

But Don't Forget God!
✦ ✦ ✦

It is worth noting here that along with the covenant of blessing comes a warning: **But thou shalt remember the Lord thy God** (v. 18). If we look back at the previous verses in Deuteronomy 8:11-14,17, then we can get an even fuller picture of the warning:

> Beware that thou forget not the Lord thy God.... Lest when thou hast eaten and art full, and hast built goodly houses, and dwelt therein; and when thy herds and thy flocks multiply, and thy silver and thy gold is multiplied, and all that thou hast is multiplied; then thine heart be lifted up....
>
> And thou say in thine heart, My power and the might of mine hand hath gotten me this wealth.

Obviously, this warning is something to pay attention to and be on our guard about so that we can prevent this situation from occurring in our own lives. Also notice that God said all of the riches mentioned in these verses—from houses, to gold and silver, to everything we have—would be multiplied!

Listen, when we start getting riches and all of the things that come along with them, then the temptation will come for us to spend so much time playing with all of our "things" that our time with God gets stolen. The homes, cars, boats, planes, campers, golf clubs, computers, televisions, games and other "toys" aren't for us to set our hearts upon. They are merely a display of God's love for us and to make our lives more enjoyable. When we get a true revelation of this, "things" won't distract us from walking with God, and our affections will be on heavenly things, not earthly things, enabling us to enjoy having things and sharing them with others.

Meet the Needs of the Body of Christ
✦ ✦ ✦

The third reason God wants us to prosper financially is so that we can help meet the needs in the body of Christ.

This third reason is very closely associated with the second reason, because meeting the needs of Christians is always tied in with spreading the Gospel, the Good News about God's love.

One verse in particular talks about meeting those needs:

But whoso hath this world's good, and seeth his brother have need, and shutteth up his bowels of compassion from him, how dwelleth the love of God in him?

—1 JOHN 3:17

Notice that giving is connected with your displaying the love of God in your life. You could say it this way: "Your giving is the proof that you love God!" We see this same truth in 2 Corinthians 8, verses 8 and 24. It is so easy for people to say they love God, but the verses in Corinthians as well as our verse here in 1 John are telling us to "put our money where our mouths are!"

This verse also tells us that if we possess the financial means to help our brothers in Christ, then we should make the sacrifices necessary to help them. I like the way *The Message* Bible reads: **...we ought to live sacrificially for our fellow believers, and not just be out for ourselves. If you see some brother or sister in need and have the means to do something about it but turn a cold shoulder and do nothing, what happens to God's love? It disappears. And you made it disappear.**

Well, according to all the Scriptures we have looked at so far, God does want us to have this world's possessions in our hands. In fact, He tells us in Ephesians 4:28 that we are supposed to work good jobs so that we can have the means to help those facing needs. So, these verses show us that God wants all of our needs met with plenty left over to help others. And although these verses primarily talk about meeting the needs of those in the body of Christ, God is also concerned about meeting the needs of the poor.

Give to the Poor

✦ ✦ ✦

The fourth reason God desires for us to be wealthy is so we can give to the poor. Giving to the poor shouldn't be taken lightly, as God takes it very seriously. When He refers to the poor in the following Scriptures, the individual writers were talking to the children of Israel, telling them to take care of the poor within their own nation. However, under the New Testament, we can give to the poor in conjunction with preaching the Gospel to every creature, Christian and non-Christian alike! We need to tell struggling Christians that God has provided a way out of their poverty and tell sinners that God loves them and has an abundant life waiting for them.

Now, let's notice what the following verses say that God will do for those of us who give to the poor:

Blessed is he that considereth the poor: the Lord will deliver him in time of trouble.

—PSALM 41:1

He that hath pity upon the poor lendeth unto the Lord; and that which he hath given will he pay him again.

—PROVERBS 19:17

He that hath a bountiful eye shall be blessed;
for he giveth of his bread to the poor.

—PROVERBS 22:9

He that giveth unto the poor shall not lack.

—PROVERBS 28:27

Wow! Giving to the poor will move God to deliver us from trouble, pay us back, bless us and free us from lack. When we give provision to the poor, then He will increase our provision. It is a win-win situation!

Other Scriptures tell us even more about giving to the poor. We see that giving to the poor honors God (Prov. 14:31), shows that we obey and fear God (Ps. 112:9), is something that Jesus and His disciples did (John 13:29) and was a practice of the early church (Rom. 15:26).

God Remembers You

✦ ✦ ✦

As I said earlier, God wants you blessed financially and materially because you are His child and He loves you. That is His first and foremost reason for prosperity. But someone may still be thinking, *Well, I don't know. If we preach that, people will want riches only for themselves.* That is simply not true! In fact, just the opposite will happen.

When people get a revelation of God's love for them and the covenant that He has made with them, they will never get lifted up in pride, thinking that they are the ones who got themselves all the wealth. On the contrary, they will think about how much God loves them every time a financial blessing comes their way, and they will want to get the Good News out to everyone about the love of God and how much He cares about them.

That is exactly what happened to my wife and me. Once we really understood why God wanted us to prosper, it freed us up to give. Now we are established in the fact that He wants to prosper us; first of all, because He loves us; secondly, because He wants us to spread His Gospel; thirdly, so that we can give to meet the needs of the body of Christ; and finally, so we can give to those who are poor.

Ever since we received this revelation, our giving has continued to climb, which in turn has caused more increase to come. His grace is abounding toward us more and more! Now nobody, not even the devil, can make us feel guilty when we buy something expensive for ourselves because we know that God loves us, and He wants us to have it. We no longer yield to any fear of lack because we know the source of our provision. This frees us up to always stay ready to give to others so that the Gospel can be spread and God's wonderful covenant can be established in people's lives!

I believe with all my heart that if we will continually remind ourselves of these reasons that God wants us to prosper, then it will keep our hearts and motives pure and holy as God blesses us with an abundance of wealth.

I don't know about you and your family, but I know about me and mine, and we are convinced that this biblical doctrine needs to be taught to the entire body of Christ. It will cause *God* to have first place in our lives, open the door for His *gold* to flow into our financial situations and give us the opportunity to produce fruit in our lives that will bring Him all of the *glory!*

✦ ✦ ✦

MONEY IS GOOD!

We have seen from God's Word that it is His will for us to prosper and to have wealth. So why is it that riches *seem* to cause so much heartache and evil? Now, I know that some people believe that riches *are* the cause, and they will even go around saying, "Money is the root of all evil." But that simply isn't true, because that isn't what the Bible teaches!

The Root of All Evil
✦ ✦ ✦

Let's go over to 1 Timothy 6:10 and see what the Scriptures really say: **For the love of money is the root of all evil: which while some coveted after, they have erred from the faith, and pierced themselves through with many sorrows.** Notice that the Bible doesn't say money is the root of all evil. It says that *the love of money* is the root of all evil!

Money is an inanimate object. It can be used for good, and it can be used for evil. But that doesn't change the money. Just because some people use money for evil doesn't make money evil. Someone may walk over and pick up a stick lying on the ground and say, "This stick is evil." If asked why he said that, he may respond, "Because I saw someone pick it up and hit a man on the head and kill him." You would immediately think, *No, the stick isn't evil. The man that used it is evil.* Likewise, it isn't money that is evil; it is the people who use it who are evil.

Do you remember what God said in Genesis 1:31 after He finished creating everything? He looked at it all and said, "This is very good!" Do you know what that means? In God's eyes, money and things are good! Yes, that is what I said. Money is good! God never intended for money to be used for evil any more than He intended for the rest of His creation to be used for evil. Man is the one who got it all messed up!

Godliness Is Gain
✦ ✦ ✦

Years ago, as a baby Christian, I was endeavoring to humble myself before the Lord and said something to this effect: "Lord, I don't want any of this world's goods or riches. After all, You said we didn't bring any of it into the world, and we can't take any of it when we go." I had been taught in church that the verses preceding 1 Timothy 6:10 meant that it wasn't God's will for Christians to have much wealth. They read as follows:

> But godliness with contentment is great gain. For we brought nothing into this world, and it is certain we can carry nothing out. And having food and raiment let us be therewith content. But

they that will be rich fall into temptation and a snare, and into many foolish and hurtful lusts, which drown men in destruction and perdition.

—1 TIMOTHY 6:6-9

Do you know that the Lord refused to receive my false humility? Here is what He said to me: "I didn't create all the riches for you to bring in or take out of the world. I created them for you to use while you are there!" And with my lightning fast mind I thought, *Duh! I should have been able to figure that one out on my own!*

Someone might be thinking, *Well, what about verse 8, which tells you to be content with food and clothing?* Again, this verse has been taken out of its context and made to say something that it isn't saying. After all, if it really were saying that, we should be content with just food and clothing; we shouldn't want a home or a car. That means we shouldn't want televisions, radios, cassette players, telephones, animals, lawnmowers, furniture, toys for the children or anything else! Jesus should have been content with food and clothing and slept on the ground rather than living in a house in Capernaum. And He should have walked into Jerusalem rather than riding on a donkey! Well, you can see very quickly that interpreting verse 8 like that is totally silly and unscriptural.

The key, once again, is to read the verse in its context. If you will read verses 3-5, you will find that they refer to men who don't consent to the Word of God and its teachings. They think that financial and material gain is a sign of godliness. It tells you to withdraw yourselves from those kinds of people. Then verse 6 says, **But godliness with contentment is great gain.**

The Greek word for *godliness* also means "piety." Following the Greek definitions further, as well as looking in Webster's Dictionary, we see that *piety* means holiness and reverence with regard to the Gospel message. Simply stated, it is talking about living our lives according to the message and doctrine contained in the Word of God.

The Greek word for *contentment* means "self-satisfaction."[1] In other words, when you are following after godliness by obeying the Word of God, you have a sense of satisfaction, peace and rest within yourself.

Now look at the words *great gain*. The Greek word for *gain* means "(a way, i.e. means), furnishing (procuring), i.e. (by impl.) money-getting (acquisition), gain."[2] It is the same Greek word used in the previous verse where it tells us that people who are ungodly and don't know the truth think that pretending to be godly will be a means to financial gain. The *New Translation* puts it this way: **These people always cause trouble. Their minds are corrupt, and they don't tell the truth. To them, religion is just a way to get rich** (Barclay). So, in context, this word *gain* here in verse 6 indicates a way or a means of procuring, or acquiring, money. The word for *great* means "big."[3] We get the prefix *mega* from this Greek word, as it refers to something that is huge. In other words, this is a way, or means, of receiving large amounts of wealth.

So what is God telling us in these verses? He is telling us that financial gain is not the means to godliness, but that godliness will furnish financial gain. And if we will follow after godliness by obeying and walking according to the Word of God, then the acquisition of great amounts of wealth will be the by-product, and our contentment will come from walking with God, not from getting things.

So, when verse 8 tells us to be content with food and clothing, it isn't telling us that we can't have other things. It is telling us that our satisfaction shouldn't depend on getting more things: Our satisfaction and contentment should be in God.

What About Those Who Aren't Content?
✦ ✦ ✦

According to verse 9, they will fall into all kinds of evil: **But they that will be rich fall into temptation and a snare, and into many foolish and hurtful lusts, which drown men in destruction and perdition.**

The words *they that will be rich* refer to the people mentioned in verses 3 through 5. They are the ones who love money more than they are longing for God. They don't submit to the Word. Therefore, it says they know nothing, and they are destitute of the truth.

That brings us back to verse 10, which says,

> **For the love of money is the root of all evil: which while some coveted after, they have erred from the faith, and pierced themselves through with many sorrows.**

Again, I will point out that money isn't the problem! This verse reveals that it is the love of money, or the coveting of money, that is the problem. The Greek word for *coveted* means "to stretch oneself" and can be stated, more simply, to "reach out after" or "long for."[4] Obviously, in this context, it is talking about people who love money. So, they are longing after money more than they are longing for God. And look what happens when they do: **They have erred from the faith, and pierced themselves through with many sorrows** (v. 10).

In other words, they have been led astray from God and His Word and opened themselves up to grief and sorrow. If they had been prospering the way God teaches in His Word, God's blessings would have come, and no sorrow would have been added with it.

Covetousness Brings Discontent
✦ ✦ ✦

First Timothy isn't the only place that we are warned about covetousness. Jesus speaks about it in Luke 12:15 as well: **And he said unto them, Take heed, and beware of covetousness: for a man's life consisteth not in the abundance of the things which he possesseth.**

People have said through the years that we shouldn't desire to have more riches; and if we do, then it is a sign of covetousness. But that simply isn't true. Let me show you why.

First of all, if it is God's will for us to have wealth, then it can't be wrong to desire what God wants us to have. Since it brings Him pleasure when we receive His prosperity into our lives, we should want to prosper. That isn't covetousness. That is righteousness!

Secondly, if you will look up the Greek word used for *covetousness,* you will find that it literally means "a desire to have more" and is always used in a bad, or evil, sense.[5] In this verse, it refers specifically to material possessions and involves extortion. Covetousness uses wrong means to attain wealth, holds onto it for selfish reasons, then wants more, thinking it will bring contentment.

But the verse goes on to tell us that our lives don't consist of the abundance of our possessions. In other words, we shouldn't look to our possessions to give us life; we should look to Jesus! That is why Jesus gives the warning, **Take heed, and beware of covetousness...**(v. 15).

For Jesus to make this statement indicates to me that all of us are going to be tempted to covet riches. The verse doesn't say, "Take heed and beware of covetousness, you rich people." No, this verse doesn't exclude anybody. As a matter of fact, you can be poor and covet money, thinking that you will never be content without having more. This verse may even be talking to you because you may be thinking that content- ment comes from things, rather than from God. Therefore, every single one of us, whether rich, poor or somewhere in between, needs to be on guard against covetousness.

The wonderful thing about this Scripture is that it will encourage those of us who want to walk in the riches that Jesus paid the price for us to have. Let me explain. Notice Jesus said, **Take heed, and beware...**(v. 15). Paraphrasing from the Greek into modern English, you could say it this way: "Pay attention and be on your guard so you can avoid covetousness!"

Let me illustrate. If you were coming over to my home for dinner and I told you that I had a big, vicious attack dog and that you should take heed and beware of him, does that mean I want you to be eaten by my dog? No! If I had wanted you to get eaten by him, I wouldn't say anything about him. I would just say, "Come on over for dinner." But I said, "Take heed and beware of my attack dog." So what am I telling you? I'm telling you to pay attention and be on your guard so that you can avoid being my dog's dinner!

That is what Jesus is telling us in this verse: "Pay attention and be on your guard so you can avoid covetousness!" That is exciting because Jesus is telling us that even though we will be tempted to covet, we can avoid it.

Now, let's go back to the verse in 1 Timothy 6:10 and see if anyone avoided covetousness: **For the love of money is the root of all evil: which while some coveted after, they have erred from the faith, and pierced themselves through with many sorrows.** Notice it doesn't say *many* coveted after it. It doesn't say *most* coveted after it. It says only *some* of them coveted after it. That means that many, or most, of them didn't! They were the ones who paid attention and kept their guard up so they could avoid it.

Watch Out for Pitfalls

✦ ✦ ✦

In 1 Timothy 6:17 Paul gives even further instruction on the subject: **Charge them that are rich in this world, that they be not highminded, nor trust in uncertain riches, but in the living God, who giveth us richly all things to enjoy.**

Like the other verse we looked at in Timothy, this one is written to Christians as well; but it specifically addresses those who are rich. The Greek word for *rich* means "abundantly, richly."[6] It refers literally to "(the) rich."[7] So apparently there were Christians with riches who were *in* this world but not *of* this world. Notice, he doesn't scold them for being rich or tell them to get rid of it all; instead, he warns them about a couple of pitfalls that will open them up to covetousness. Let's look at them.

The first is that they ...**be not highminded** (v. 17). To be *high-minded* is "to be lofty in mind."[8] Another way of saying it is "to be arrogant." In other words, don't let your money change the way you act toward people. Don't think you are better than someone else because you live in a bigger house, drive a better car or wear better clothes. That is being high-minded.

The second warning is to not trust in uncertain riches. The word *trust* means "to expect or confide."[9] In other words, if you think that you will finally be happy when you get the new home, buy the new car or join a certain club, then your expectation, confidence and hope are in the wrong place. Remember, Jesus said you shouldn't look to things to give you life and fulfillment. And *things* are what make up riches—things like real estate, gems, businesses, gold, silver, cars, stocks, homes, etc.

There is an uncertainty about riches because they are finicky. They may be worth a lot today and lose their value tomorrow. The dollar is up one day and down the next. Real estate prices soar to the sky, and then the bottom falls out. Interest rates are all over the place. That is why he refs to them as *uncertain riches,* and that is why we should keep our hope and confidence in God and His system, because it is a sure thing. There is no uncertainty about God's plan of prosperity!

Place Your Confidence in God
✦ ✦ ✦

So where do we keep our expectation, confidence and hope? First Timothy 6:17 says ...**in the living God, who giveth us richly all things to enjoy.** Keeping our trust in God means that we are staying full of His Word and obeying everything He tells us to do. When we do, then He will abundantly provide us with everything for our enjoyment. Notice that the verse tells us that He gives us all things to enjoy, not love. In other words, we can have and enjoy riches without loving them. Isn't God awesome? Not only did He make a way through Jesus for us to be financially free, but He also told us that no matter how rich we become we are capable of keeping our trust in Him so that we can fully enjoy our financial freedom. He truly is a wonderful God.

CHAPTER 9

✦ ✦ ✦

TWO SYSTEMS OF PROSPERITY

"So if money is good, then why do so many ungodly and wicked people seem to have it in their possession?" The answer is very simple: There are two systems of prosperity operating in this world—the devil's system and God's system. Unfortunately, many Christians have unknowingly been operating under the devil's system of economics rather than God's.

The Result of God's System
✦ ✦ ✦

However, back in our first chapter, we looked in Ephesians 2 and Romans 12 and found out that we, as Christians, don't have to be guided by the devil's system, which is operating in this world. We have been translated into God's kingdom, which means even though we are in this world we are not of this world. Therefore, we can operate by a whole different set of rules.

When we operate within God's system of prosperity, the wealth that comes to us won't bring us sorrow; instead, it will bring us blessing. Look at Proverbs 10:22: **The** blessing of the Lord, it maketh rich, and he addeth no sorrow with it. Paraphrasing that from the Hebrew it could read: "The prosperity that comes from the Lord will bring us wealth, and He will add no trouble with it." In other words, when we prosper according to God's system, then God's blessings will be upon us and not the curses that go along with the devil's system.

The Result of the World's System

✦ ✦ ✦

Solomon spoke about the devil's, or the world's, system of prosperity in Proverbs 1:32. I believe Solomon had a right to speak on prosperity because God had given him an abundance of wealth! Look at what he said in that verse: **The prosperity of fools shall destroy them.**

When you read the whole context here you find that the word *fools* refers to people who have chosen their own ways and the world's ways of doing things and not God's ways. He is talking about ungodly people who prosper according to the world's system. And He says that kind of prosperity will end up destroying them.

"Well, Brother Larry, I know some ungodly people who are rich, and they are living the good life. In fact, they are getting away with murder and nothing bad seems to be happening to them!" That may seem the way it is, but according to God their wealth will end up destroying them. For further light on this, let's look at Psalm 73.

The Prosperity of the Wicked
✦ ✦ ✦

This Psalm talks about the world's system of prosperity. The writer here is Asaph. Asaph was a Levite and a chief musician. Second Chronicles 29:30 calls him the seer. The Hebrew word for *seer* also means "prophet."[1] In fact, Asaph's name means "collector."[2] Asaph would collect, or receive, words from God and speak them forth in song or write them down. That is what he did here in this Psalm. Let me quote a portion of it: **For I was envious at the foolish, when I saw the prosperity of the wicked** (Ps. 73:3).

Asaph found himself envying their riches. He continues in verses 4-9, 11:

> **For there are no bands in their death: but their strength is firm. They are not in trouble as other men; neither are they plagued like other men. Therefore pride compasseth them about as a chain; violence covereth them as a garment. Their eyes stand out with fatness: they have more than heart could wish. They are corrupt, and speak wickedly concerning oppression: they speak loftily. They set their mouth against the heavens, and their tongue walketh through the earth.**
>
> **And they say, How doth God know? and is there knowledge in the most High?**

Notice Asaph said in verse 3 that he began envying them and then explains why in verses 4-11. He said they had no struggles. They were strong and healthy. They were free from the burdens and ills that other men faced. They

wore pride as you would jewelry and violence like clothing. They were always looking for more, and they already
had an abundance. They said whatever they wanted to say
no matter who it hurt or how evil it was, and their mouths
continually said things against the heavens and the earth.

Then in verse 11, they even started mocking and
making fun of God. But notice what Asaph said about
them in verse 12: **Behold, these are the ungodly, who
prosper in the world; they increase in riches**. So apparently there is a system of prosperity in this world whereby
you can get rich, but God has nothing to do with it.

Asaph went on to say in verse 16: **When I thought to
know this, it was too painful for me.** Asaph admitted here
that the more he thought about these ungodly, wicked
people and their wealth, the more jealous he got. Asaph
was jealous because they had so much prosperity, and they
were getting away with murder, or so it seemed. Asaph was
suffering mental and emotional pain until he went into the
sanctuary of God and understood their end. (v. 17.)

The Ultimate End of the Ungodly
✦ ✦ ✦

In other words, once Asaph got on his face before God
about the situation, God allowed the prophet to see what
would sooner or later happen to these people who were
operating in the world's system of prosperity. He reveals it
in verses 18 and 19.

**Surely thou didst set them in slippery places:
thou castedst them down into destruction. How**

**are they brought into desolation, as in a moment!
they are utterly consumed with terrors.**

Notice the words *slippery places, destruction, desolation,
in a moment* and *consumed with terrors.* How many times in
recent years have we seen those very things happening to
millionaires and billionaires who aren't godly people? One
day one of them is out on his yacht, and he somehow falls
overboard and drowns. Another one is found dead in his
bed from an apparent heart attack. Another one is
murdered. Another one loses his millions overnight and
commits suicide. Another one is found dead from an over-
dose. Another is struck down by a disease, and his life is
terminated. And still another is so terrified by germs that
he can't even leave his home.

Listen, friends, it isn't the money that is causing those
things to happen. It is the system within which they are
operating and attaining their money. Have you ever heard
someone say, "This is a dog-eat-dog world"? Well, what
they mean is that the world's system is set up so that you
are on your own. People in general don't care about
anybody but themselves. They want to climb the ladder of
success more quickly than you, even if it means stepping
on your head to do it!

They try to work all their lives to make enough so
they can enjoy retirement. They live from paycheck to
paycheck. They save, save, save and make all they can—
and can all they make, and then they put a lid on the can!
You can even hear them say, "I'm saving for a rainy day."
Then when the rainy day comes, they lose all of their life's

savings. It is a sad way to live, and yet many Christians are living that way.

This world's system wasn't designed for the children of God. The world's system of economics is just the opposite of God's system. It will bring failure, heartache, disappointment, discouragement, discontentment, confusion, helplessness, envying, strife, covetousness and, most of all, it will keep you out of fellowship with your heavenly Father.

Go With God

✦ ✦ ✦

Unfortunately, not enough Christians are operating according to God's system of prosperity, and the wealth has gotten into the wrong hands. Nevertheless, God says in Proverbs 13:22 that the sinners can't keep the wealth because ...**the wealth of the sinner is laid up for the just.** In other words, He will take the riches out of the sinners' hands and bring them into the possession of the righteous. And since all of the wealth belongs to Him anyway, He can freely give it to any of His children who are willing and obedient to operate within His system.

In Ecclesiastes 2:26 NIV, Solomon says,

> **To the man who pleases him, God gives wisdom, knowledge and happiness, but to the sinner he gives the task of gathering and storing up wealth to hand it over to the one who pleases God.**

This verse gives us some insight into what Solomon thought about the wealth of the sinner. He says that God has the sinners working for and storing up wealth to hand over to those of us who are pleasing Him.

This, of course, goes right along with Proverbs 13:22: **A good man leaveth an inheritance to his children's children: and the wealth of the sinner is laid up for the just.** Notice this verse calls a good man "the just." The *New Translation* says it this way: **Good people leave an inheritance to their grandchildren, but the sinner's wealth passes to the godly** (Barclay). A good man, therefore, is a godly man; and he is supposed to leave an inheritance to his grandchildren. What is the inheritance he is supposed to leave? Is it just a little gift or small part of an estate? No, it is the sinner's wealth! God didn't say the sinner's poverty and lack would be transferred to the righteous; He said it would be the sinner's wealth! This Scripture further illustrates God's willingness for His children to be wealthy.

Once we have an understanding of God's Word in this area, then we can readily see that money and wealth aren't the problem. The problem has been Christians not following God's system of prosperity. And now that we have become aware of the two systems of prosperity that are operating in this world, we no longer have to shy away from prosperity, but just from the world's way of prospering. As long as we operate in the world's system, we have no legal means to attain riches. But when we operate according to God's system, through Jesus and what He accomplished at Calvary, we then have legal means and a God-given right to obtain great wealth. Let's put God first in our finances and operate in His system—the results will bring Him honor and glory!

Part III

THE GLORY

◆ ◆ ◆

CHAPTER 10

✦ ✦ ✦

GOD'S SYSTEM OF PROSPERITY

So exactly what is God's system of prosperity? It is a system that operates completely independently of the world's system. It is not based on our circumstances or what is happening in our nation's economy. It is not founded upon the types of jobs we have, our educations, backgrounds, nationalities or ages. God's system of prosperity is no respecter of persons and will work for every child of God who will practice it in his daily life. So it doesn't matter whether there is a recession or a depression, because His system operates out of *His* riches in glory.

God's system is not a get-rich-quick scheme; it is a way of life. There are no formulas to figure out, no levers to pull or buttons to push. In fact, there are only two requirements for becoming financially free within God's system. First of all, we have to have a relationship with God. This comes only through the new birth. Jesus said unless a man is born again he cannot enter the kingdom of God. (John 3:3-5.) Once we are born of the Spirit, we then have the ability to operate according to His system. Secondly, we must maintain a close fellowship with God if we expect Him to lead and guide us in His paths of prosperity. When we look at the great patriarchs of the Bible such as Abraham, Isaac, Jacob, Joseph, David, Solomon and others, we see that as long as they put God first in their lives He made them prosper.

Therefore, if we are going to prosper today the way God wants us to, then we have to put Him first in our lives and walk in close fellowship with Him by hearing and doing all that He says in His Word. When we do, then according to James 1:25, everything we put our hands to will prosper.

One thing is absolutely sure: God's system of financial prosperity is the best system available on the earth today— bar none! However, you have to have that truth established in *your* heart by the Word of God.

The Promise

✦ ✦ ✦

God's Word is full of instructions concerning money. And because many of us have been religiously brainwashed instead of biblically taught, it is time to renew our minds with the Word of God and get rid of what I call our "stinking thinking." Let's look, first of all, at Proverbs 3:9-10:

> **Honour the Lord with thy substance, and
> with the firstfruits of all thine increase: So shall
> thy barns be filled with plenty, and thy presses
> shall burst out with new wine.**

Verse 9 tells us what we are supposed to do, while verse 10 tells us what the result will be or what God will do for us because of our obedience. Notice, first of all, the result in verse 10: **So shall thy barns be filled with plenty, and thy presses shall burst out with new wine.**

The Hebrew word for *barns* means "storehouses."[1] Barns and storehouses always refer to the places where the excess is kept. It is interesting to note here that the word *barns* appears in the plural. So He is talking not only about one barn being filled, but more than one barn! Now, if we were going to put this in modern-day language, we might substitute the words "bank accounts" or "investments," because those are our storehouses. The word *plenty,* which describes how the barns are to be filled, means "abundance."[2] So, in modern-day language, God is letting us know in this verse that He wants our bank accounts filled with abundance!

The next portion of this same verse is similar to the first portion. In this portion, He adds **...and thy presses shall burst out with new wine** (v. 10). This statement refers to the vats that were used to catch the fresh grape juice that was just squeezed. Growing grapes was a business. Well, we may not be in that type of business, but if God promised overflowing blessings for their businesses, then it would still apply to us today!

Paraphrasing this verse, it could read, "It will come to pass that God will fill your bank accounts with abundance and cause your jobs and businesses to burst with overflowing blessings!"

The Condition

✦ ✦ ✦

The fulfillment of this verse in our lives, however, depends upon our willingness to obey verse 9: **Honour**

the Lord with thy substance, and with the firstfruits of all thine increase. But what does it mean to honor the Lord? The word *honor* here is a verb, implying that we *do* something. On numerous occasions this Hebrew word is translated "glorify," meaning that we should do something to honor or glorify Him. Another definition of this Hebrew word is to "promote." And if you stop and think about it, promoting the Lord in our lives is what brings honor and glory to Him. Promoting the Lord means to live like He wants us to live, thereby producing fruit in our lives that will glorify Him. Jesus stated in Matthew 5:16, **Let your light so shine before men, that they may see your good works, and glorify your Father which is in heaven.** Notice, this verse says we do something that will glorify our Father. What do we do? We let our lights shine to people so that when they observe our deeds and actions they give glory to God. That means we are promoting God in our lives. Jesus made a similar statement in John 15:8: **Herein is my Father glorified, that ye bear much fruit; so shall ye be my disciples.** He tells us here that we glorify God when we bear much fruit. Bearing fruit, doing good works and letting our light shine is the way we promote God in our lives and cause Him to be honored and glorified. I personally like to use the definition "promote" here in Proverbs 3:9 because I believe it makes it easier to understand the verse.

So, God wants us to *do* something to promote Him that will bring Him honor and glory. What does this verse tell us to do? It tells us to promote the Lord with our substance and the firstfruits of our increase. Another word for *substance* is "wealth."[3] This is what you actually own or have in your possession. In other words, everything that belongs to you is your wealth, and you are to give of it to the Lord.

The next thing mentioned is the *firstfruits of all our increase.* The Hebrew word for *firstfruits* means "beginning," "chief" or "first."[4] And the word for *increase* means "income."[5]

Notice, we are told to promote the Lord in two ways—with the wealth that already belongs to us and with the first part of all the money we receive. Promoting the Lord with the first part of our income is called *tithes.* Promoting the Lord with our substance is called *offerings.*

So, in a very real sense, when we choose to promote God with our tithes and our offerings, we are bringing honor and glory to Him.

When we tithe and give offerings to a local church that is getting people saved, filled, healed, delivered and set free, then we are promoting the Lord. When we support the traveling ministers who are helping the local churches and changing the lives of people, we are promoting the Lord. When we support missionaries who are changing other countries, we are promoting the Lord. When we help send Bibles into the world, we are promoting the Lord. When we send materials into the prisons so that inmates can be set free, we are promoting the Lord. When we support outreaches to the poor that are preaching the Gospel, we are promoting the Lord. When we support men and women with life-changing messages on Christian television and radio, we are promoting the Lord.

I could go on and on, but I believe that is enough for us to understand what our tithes and offerings are supposed to do. We are supposed to pay tithes and give offerings to honor the Lord; and when we do, it brings Him glory.

That is the way God's kingdom is supposed to be financed on the earth—not by bake sales, barbecues, bazaars or car washes! Those are good for groups to raise money for trips, but churches and ministries ought to be operating in abundance because of the body's faithfulness in the paying of tithes and in the giving of offerings.

If you do what the Scriptures tell you to do and give of your tithes and your offerings, then the *so shall* of verse 10 will come to pass, and God will bless you by pouring His abundance into your life.

The Tithe

✦ ✦ ✦

Let's talk about the tithe first. We are told in Leviticus 27:30, **And all the tithe of the land, whether of the seed of the land, or of the fruit of the tree, is the Lord's: it is holy unto the Lord.** To whom does this verse say all the tithe belongs? To the Lord! It also calls the tithe "holy." The Hebrew definition means "apartness, holiness, sacredness, separateness."[6] In other words, the tithe is a sacred thing and has been consecrated and set apart for the service of God. Brethren, this is not something that is to be taken lightly! The tithe is a holy thing, and it belongs to the Lord! So then, what is the tithe? Both the Hebrew and the Greek define the tithe as the tenth part.[7] In other words, it is the first 10 percent of our income. When Abraham tithed to the high priest, Melchizedek, he gave him the first 10 percent right off of the top of his earnings.

(Gen. 14:20.) When Abel put God first in his life, he brought the firstlings of his flock to Him. (Gen. 4:4.) The words *firstfruits, tithe, tenth part* or *first part,* all mean "first"! In other words, God comes before anyone or anything else, including our government.

So does that mean we are to tithe based upon our gross income or our net income? I encourage you to always adhere to what the Bible says. God wants us to put Him first, not after Uncle Sam, not after our mortgage payment, not after our bills, not after our golf game or shopping spree. God wants us to put Him first, then He will make sure we have plenty left over for all of those other things.

"But, Brother Larry, I've been tithing based upon my net income because I heard that when we get our paycheck, the taxes are already taken out. And since we never see that, then we don't have to tithe on the gross." Let me remind you that Proverbs 3:9 tells us to tithe from *our* income. That would include monies received from gifts, inheritances and settlements, as well as our jobs. What would *our* income be from our jobs?

Well, in our country, when you accept a job and your employer sits down with you and tells you how much you are going to make, does he tell you your gross income or your net? He tells you what *your* income will be before taxes are taken out. Why? Because it is *your* income. In fact, to further prove that it is *yours,* he will have you fill out a W-4 form, and on that form you have to decide how much tax you want withheld from *your* paychecks. Of course, the more deductions that you claim, the less tax is withheld. Do you know why you have a say-so in that? Because it is *your* income!

Just because your government requires you to pay taxes doesn't mean that you put them first. If you are going to do that in one area, then you ought to be figuring out how much state tax, sales tax, property tax and all the other taxes that your government is requiring you to pay, and then pay tithes after all those are deducted. Can you see how foolish this is?

Yes, your government requires you to pay taxes, but your God also requires you to pay tithes. So the best thing to do is to do just what the Bible says: **Render therefore unto Caesar the things which are Caesar's; and unto God the things that are God's** (Matt. 22:21).

We will cover the tithe in more detail in the next chapter, but let's talk about the offering for a moment.

The Offering
✦ ✦ ✦

If you go back to Proverbs 3:9, you will see that the tithe and the offering are mentioned together. The tithe is the first 10 percent of the income and belongs to God, but what about the offering?

In order to truly give an offering to the Lord, you must first tithe; then whatever you give above that is considered your offering. Unfortunately, some people have been taught that when they take the first 10 percent of their income to the local church that they have given. But, in reality, they haven't given anything! They have simply brought what belonged to God to its rightful owner. In order to really give, you must give of what belongs to you, and since the tithe doesn't belong to you, then it can't be given as an offering. Everything that remains after you have tithed belongs to you and is what you use to give offerings to the Lord.

How much are you supposed to give? Actually the Scriptures don't indicate a specific amount. All that He asks is that you give something that belongs to you and that you give it from your heart.

Now, that isn't to say that God won't speak to you about giving a certain amount to someone. I have had Him do that with me. In fact, I have seen from the Scriptures and my own personal experience that God usually deals with me about giving in two ways. Either He tells me to give a certain amount that I already have and can give right now, or He deals with me about giving a certain amount that I have to believe Him for before I can give it; that is called giving beyond your ability.

Most likely, He will deal with you in much the same way. But either way, you can be absolutely and positively sure of this one thing: If you want to experience increase in your life, then you are going to have to give "big." There is just no way around it.

"But, Brother Larry, I'm poor and don't have much to give. How am I going to experience increase?"

You say you don't have much to give? Who told you that? God didn't. The Bible indicates that your giving should be in proportion to what you have. It isn't so much the amount that counts as it is the proportion. Let me give you a biblical example about some rich men and a widow who were casting their gifts into the treasury at the temple:

> And he looked up, and saw the rich men casting their gifts into the treasury. And he saw also a certain poor widow casting in thither two mites. And he said, Of a truth I say unto you, that this poor widow hath cast in more than they all: For all these have of their abundance cast in unto the offerings of God: but she of her penury hath cast in all the living that she had.
>
> —LUKE 21:1-4

It says she cast in of her *penury*. The Greek word means "deficit" and refers specifically to "poverty."[8] In other words, if anyone couldn't afford to give, she qualified. And yet Jesus said that she had cast in more than all the rest put together.

Notice how much she cast in—two mites. She gave two *lepta* (Gr.). A *lepton* was the smallest bronze Jewish coin in circulation in Palestine. Two *lepta* were worth 1/64 of a Roman denarius, a day's wage for a laborer. For his Roman readers, Mark stated their value in terms of Roman coinage, namely, **a fraction of a penny.**[9] So, in essence, she cast in just a fraction of a day's wages, which, according to Mark 12:44, was all that she had to live on. Now notice how much the others cast in. Mark 12:41 says that many rich people cast in much; and yet, look at what Jesus said in verse 43: ...**I say unto you, That this poor widow hath cast more in, than all they which have cast into the treasury.**

I'm sure that if these rich people would have given a significant proportion of their income Jesus would have bragged on them as much as He bragged on her. For Him to brag on her giving and not theirs tells me that they didn't give much in proportion to what they had. The amounts that they gave actually amounted to more in the natural than what she gave, but God said that this woman's offering was the one that qualified as big giving.

The rest of the story about what happened to this woman isn't recorded here. But I would suspect that she received a tremendous return on her giving. In other words, she probably wasn't poor anymore!

Regardless of how much or how little you have, everyone has something to give. It doesn't matter if you are the poorest person in the world. You have something to give. This woman was poor, but she didn't stay that way. Like this woman, you have to start where you are; then trust God to take you where He wants you to be.

✦ ✦ ✦

IS TITHING FOR TODAY?

Sometimes Christians try tithing without the faith to do it, which causes their actions to be a work of the law instead of a work of righteousness based upon faith. Then they approach tithing as a drudgery and a pain, and they end up pulling Scriptures out of context to try to prove that they don't have to tithe.

One of these false proofs is that tithing isn't for us today because we are under the new covenant. They say it was a part of the law, and since we aren't under the law but under grace, then we don't have to tithe.

What About Abraham?
✦ ✦ ✦

But wait a minute! Didn't Abraham tithe, and didn't he live long before the law was given? Let's take a look at the two accounts that talk about Abraham tithing. One is in Genesis, and the other is in the book of Hebrews.

And Melchizedek king of Salem brought forth bread and wine: and he was the priest of the most

high God. And he blessed him, and said, Blessed be Abram of the most high God, possessor of heaven and earth: And blessed be the most high God, which hath delivered thine enemies into thy hand. And he gave him tithes of all.

—GENESIS 14:18-20

For this Melchisedec, king of Salem, priest of the most high God, who met Abraham returning from the slaughter of the kings, and blessed him; to whom also Abraham gave a tenth part of all.

—HEBREWS 7:1,2

We can see from both Genesis and Hebrews that Abraham was a tither, and he lived approximately 430 years before the Mosaic Law was even instituted! In other words, tithing was instituted long before the law ever existed.

From Generation to Generation
✦ ✦ ✦

But Abraham wasn't the only one who tithed before the law was instituted. His grandson, Jacob, was also a tither: **And Jacob vowed a vow...of all that thou shalt give me I will surely give the tenth unto thee** (Gen. 28:20,22).

And from whom did Jacob learn to tithe? The Bible gives us the answer to this question in the eighteenth chapter. Reading from the nineteenth verse we see something that God said about Abraham: **For I know him, that he will command his children and his household after him, and they shall keep the way of the Lord** (Gen. 18:19). Notice God said that Abraham kept His ways. Therefore, *tithing* had to have been *a way of the Lord!* Then God said that Abraham commanded his children to also follow the ways of the Lord. That lets us know that Isaac and Jacob learned to tithe from their father, Abraham, and that the ways of the Lord were passed down from generation to generation. Parents taught the principles of God to their children, and 270 years before the law was instituted, the generations of Abraham were still tithing.

This also helps us answer the next question. From whom did Abraham learn to tithe? He must have learned the ways of God from his father, Terah, his grandfather Nahor and his great-grandfather Serug. And those ways were passed down from his great-, great-, great-, great-, great-, great-, great-grandfather Noah.

Like Abraham, Noah was a man who followed the ways of God and must have learned tithing from his father, Lamech, his grandfather Methuselah and his great-grandfather Enoch. The Bible says that Enoch walked with God, so we know for sure that he was a godly man and that he followed all the ways of the Lord.

And whom did Enoch learn from? Well, he must have learned tithing from his father, Jared, his grandfather Mahalaleel, his great-grandfather Cainan and his great-, great-, great-grandfather Adam, who apparently taught his sons to tithe. Take a look at Genesis 4:1-5.

> And Adam knew Eve his wife; and she conceived, and bare Cain, and said, I have gotten a man from the Lord. And she again bare his brother Abel. And Abel was a keeper of sheep, but Cain was a tiller of the ground. And in process of

time it came to pass, that Cain brought of the fruit of the ground an offering unto the Lord. And Abel, he also brought of the firstlings of his flock and of the fat thereof. And the Lord had respect unto Abel and to his offering: But unto Cain and to his offering he had not respect.

I used to believe that the reason God wouldn't look at Cain's offering was that it wasn't a blood sacrifice, but the Lord showed me something one time that really helped me understand this passage of Scripture.

First of all, He pointed out to me that Cain was a tiller of the ground. (v. 2.) The Hebrew words used here are also found back in Genesis 2:5 where it says, **There was not a man to till the ground,** and in verse 15 where it says, **The Lord God took the man, and put him into the garden of Eden to *dress* it.** Then in Genesis 3:23, when God sent man out of the Garden because of sin, He sent him ...**to till the ground from whence he was taken.**

In other words, Cain was doing the will of God, but when it came time to bring his offering to the Lord, no mention is made that he put God first! Notice in Genesis 4:3 that **Cain brought of the fruit of the ground an offering unto the Lord.** Yes, he brought an offering, but he didn't bring of his firstfruits.

On the other hand, notice what Abel brought: **the firstlings of his flock** (v. 4). Abel put God first, and that pleased God! If Cain would have brought of the firstfruits of the ground, I believe his offering would have been just as pleasing to God as Abel's.

Furthermore, we're told in Hebrews 11:4 that it was by faith, not blood, that Abel's sacrifice was pleasing to God. Well, if it was by faith, and faith comes by hearing God's Word, then Abel's act of bringing the first of his flocks to God was obedience to God.

Now, who taught Abel to put God first in his life and bring the firstlings of his flock to the Lord? Well, the only persons it could have been were his parents, Adam and Eve. So, we must conclude that the principle of tithing began in the Garden.

Tithing Began in the Garden
✦ ✦ ✦

One time I asked the Lord, "If tithing is so important, then why isn't it spoken of more in the New Testament?" His reply to me began with a question, "Did you notice I didn't spend a lot of time in Adam's life dealing with the Tree of the Knowledge of Good and Evil? I simply told him not to eat it, and that was sufficient. He knew that it belonged to Me and that he wasn't supposed to partake of it." Then He went on to say, "Likewise the tithe is Mine, and you aren't to partake of it. So just bring it to Me."

Well, that was good enough for me, and I just decided to go ahead and do what He said! Then, as further revelation came from the Scriptures, I understood exactly what He was saying.

Let's begin in Genesis where God created man and placed him in the Garden, then told him that everything was created for his domain and that he could eat from every tree except for one!

123

> And the Lord God commanded the man, saying, Of every tree of the garden thou mayest freely eat: But of the tree of the knowledge of good and evil, thou shalt not eat of it.
>
> —GENESIS 2:16,17

Notice, there was only one thing in Adam's life that God reserved for Himself. Likewise, in our lives today, there is only one thing that God has reserved for Himself. Remember what Leviticus 27:30 says: **And all the tithe of the land...is the Lord's: it is holy unto the Lord.**

In other words, God is telling us that the first 10 percent of our income belongs to Him. And because of what Jesus did, we too have dominion over the earth, just as Adam did, so we can partake of all the good things freely except the tithe! God has reserved that for Himself.

In fact, when talking about the tithe in Deuteronomy 26:14, God essentially says not to eat the tithe. It is interesting to note that the same Hebrew word is used in Genesis 2:17 where God told Adam not to *eat* of the tree.[1] It is just as much sin for us to "eat" of the tithe (that is, to use it on ourselves) as it was for Adam to eat of the tree.

Is It Okay To Eat the Tithe?

✦ ✦ ✦

Some have said that it is okay to "eat" the tithe because God allowed the children of Israel to do it in Deuteronomy, chapters 12-14. But what we need to understand is that there are *three* different tithes spoken of in the Bible.

The first tithe spoken of was for the Levites. It was to take care of the priests as they did their service in the tabernacle. This tithe is spoken of in Leviticus 27 and Numbers 18 and is briefly alluded to in Deuteronomy 12:19 and 14:27. *This is the only tithe that we see in operation before and after the law, and it was to be eaten, or used, only by the priests.*

The second tithe that is mentioned was for the individual himself and his household. After reading Deuteronomy 12 and 14, you will find that this tithe was used to cover expenses when going to a God-appointed national gathering or feast. (Deut. 14:22-26.) Although this tithe was used, or eaten, by the individuals and their families, it didn't excuse them from paying their first tithe to the Levites. (Deut. 14:27.) God had told them to never neglect that office. (Deut. 12:19.)

The third tithe that is mentioned seems to have been more of a tithe for charity. We could call it the "third-year tithe," as it was primarily done every three years. (Deut. 14:28.) This tithe was brought into a certain place in the city and was then distributed to the Levite (priest), the stranger (traveler, guest or foreigner), the fatherless (orphan) and the widow (abandoned or forsaken woman). (Deut. 14:29.) We might also call this tithe the "compassion tithe," as one of its main purposes was to relieve suffering and lack.

The second and third tithes are only found during the time of the law. However the first tithe, the tithe to the priesthood, is the only tithe spoken of before the law and after the law. Therefore we had better adhere to it and follow in the footsteps of our father Abraham. Since he

tithed to his high priest, Melchizedek, who was a type of
Jesus, then we should tithe to our High Priest, Jesus, today!

What Is at the Center of Your Garden?

✦ ✦ ✦

Now let's go back to our comparison between the Tree
of the Knowledge of Good and Evil and the tithe. God
entrusted Adam with the tree. He put Adam in the Garden
to dress it and to keep it. (Gen. 2:15.) Even though he
couldn't use that one tree for himself, he was still instructed
to take care of it and protect it. Likewise, God has entrusted
us with the tithe. And, since it is the first 10 percent of our
income, then we have to take care of it and protect it until
we get it out of our hands.

If you will look a little more closely, you will notice
that everything in Adam's life revolved around two trees—
the Tree of Life and the Tree of the Knowledge of Good and
Evil. They were both in the middle of the Garden. (Gen.
2:9 and 3:3.) The Tree of Life was Adam's to enjoy, but the
other tree was reserved for God and God alone. However,
it too was right in the center of Adam's life. Everywhere he
went and everything he did revolved around that tree. As
long as he didn't partake of it, he could continue enjoying
abundant life, and he could partake of and enjoy all the
riches and pleasures that the world had to offer. As long as
he remained obedient, then his willingness to follow God's
instructions would be blessed!

And from that day until this, God has never changed
His mind. It is the same principle that He gave in Isaiah
1:19: **If ye be willing and obedient, ye shall eat the good**

of the land. But when that *one* instruction wasn't adhered to, all hell broke loose, and Adam found himself operating in fear, not faith. As a result, he ended up in the flesh and physical sense realm rather than the spirit realm.

Now, this may be a hard pill to swallow, but it is the truth nonetheless. The tithe is at the center of every Christian's life. If we will take care of and protect the tithe—the only thing God reserves for Himself—then God can trust us with more godly things. Whether you realize it or not, everything in your life revolves around money. Directly or indirectly, it is a part of everywhere you go and everything you do. And if you don't eat the tithe, then you can enter into God's plan of prosperity for your life and enjoy all of the riches and pleasures that God's creation affords.

Prove Yourself Faithful

✦ ✦ ✦

If you really want to walk with God the way that He wants you to, then you will have to learn to be faithful in this area. But don't take my word for it, look at what the Scriptures say in Luke 16:1-13. The whole passage talks about being faithful with money matters.

> **Therefore if you have not been faithful in the [case of] unrighteous mammon (deceitful riches, money, possessions), who will entrust to you the true riches? And if you have not proved faithful in that which belongs to another [whether God or man], who will give you that which is your own [that is, the true riches]?**

No servant is able to serve two masters; for either he will hate the one and love the other, or he will stand by and be devoted to the one and despise the other. You cannot serve God and mammon (riches, or anything in which you trust and on which you rely).

—LUKE 16:11-13 AMP

Notice what verse 12 says: **If you have not proved faithful in that which belongs to another [whether God or man]....** In other words, God is saying that if you aren't faithful with something that doesn't belong to you (i.e., the tithe), then you are serving money, not God! And if you are serving money (which you are if you aren't tithing), then you *aren't* serving God. Therefore, He won't entrust you with true riches, or as the Greek says, His (God's) riches!

Now, let's reverse that just a moment. If you are faithful in that which belongs to another (by being a tither), then you show God that you are serving Him and that He, not money, is your Master. He then can trust you with His riches, which are the true riches.

So don't buck God's system. That is what Adam did, and you can see where it got him. God didn't tell Adam not to eat of that tree to hurt him, but to help him walk in abundance. Likewise, God didn't tell you to tithe so that you would be poorer. Actually, just the opposite is true. He told you to tithe to help you walk in abundance!

Now can you see why Adam's son Abel was a tither, as well as those all the way up to our fathers—Abraham, Isaac and Jacob? It is because the principle of tithing began in the Garden and because it was a blessing to all of those who practiced it.

Tithing Is for Today
✦ ✦ ✦

So tithing is for today and was meant by God to be a blessing in your life. It is a part of His system of prosperity to bring abundance and wealth into your life. It is a part of your inheritance!

However, if you attempt to separate tithes from offerings by saying that tithing is not for us today but the giving of offerings is, then you will have to throw away the "book of wisdom" because Proverbs 3:9-10, which we have already looked at, talks about the tithe and the offering together. And, in the context of the passage, it talks about trusting God with your whole heart and walking in His ways. The results are given as health in your body and financial freedom in your life.

You will also have to throw away a portion of Malachi 3:7-9 because God talks about the ordinances of tithes and offerings that the Israelites had strayed away from since the days of their fathers. He also tells them that if they will return to the keeping of these ordinances, then He will return to them. But if the tithe isn't for us today, then the ordinance of offerings will have to be kept, but the ordinance for tithes will have to be chucked!

In addition, you will have to throw away all the Scriptures that show Abraham, Jacob and their forefathers giving tithes, which resulted in their being blessed by God with great wealth.

In the New Testament, you will have to throw away Jesus' statement in Matthew 23:23 where He called the religious people hypocrites because they were tithing and yet neglecting even more important matters of the law—judgment, mercy and faith. These all have to do with attitudes of the heart; and if they are omitted in our lives, then anything else we do won't amount to a hill of beans! Notice, the last thing mentioned was faith. Well, without faith it is impossible to please God. (Heb. 11:6.) So that means that these religious people were not exercising faith when they tithed and were therefore not pleasing God.

There is something I noticed about Jesus' teaching that needs to be pointed out here. In Matthew 5, when Jesus was teaching from the law, He addressed changes that would have to be made under the new covenant. He said repeatedly, "You have heard that it has been said...but I say unto you." (Matt. 5:21-44.) He would quote something under the law and then tell them what the change would be under the new covenant.

However, when Jesus addressed these religious people about the law in Matthew 23:23, He didn't say anything about them not tithing anymore. On the contrary, He told them that they ought to have exercised judgment, mercy and faith and not to have let tithing go undone! Well, that's concrete proof that tithing is for us under the new covenant! We are not exempt from exercising good judgment, showing mercy or using our faith, and we're not exempt from tithing either!

Another Scripture that would have to be thrown away from the New Testament, if tithing were to be rejected, is found in Romans 2:22. The latter part of the verse says, **Thou that abhorrest idols, dost thou commit sacrilege?** *The Amplified Bible* helps to shed some light on exactly what the *King James Version* means here, and it reads:

> **You who abhor and loathe idols, do you rob temples [do you appropriate to your own use what is consecrated to God, thus robbing the sanctuary and doing sacrilege]?**

Among other things, this is obviously referring to the tithe, because we know that it is holy and consecrated to God. Besides that, God calls it robbing when we don't tithe. (Mal. 3:8.) Furthermore, Ephesians 4:28 instructs Christians not to steal, and that means from God as well as from man!

You will also have to ignore Hebrews 7 and 8, which show Jesus receiving our tithes *today* as our High Priest just like Melchizedek received Abraham's tithes.

And finally, in light of the fact that Abraham tithed 430 years before the law was given, you will also have to look more closely at another New Testament Scripture found in Galatians 3:17-18 NIV.

> **What I mean is this: The law, introduced 430 years later, does not set aside the covenant previously established by God and thus do away with the promise. For if the inheritance depends on the law, then it no longer depends on a promise; but God gave it to Abraham through a promise.**

Notice that our inheritance isn't ours because of the law but because of the covenant God made with Abraham.

And the ordinances that were a part of that covenant weren't made void just because the law was instituted.

So, beware of people who come along and separate the tithe from the offering, teaching that the ordinance of tithing was under the law and, therefore, is not something that is required of us today. If you listen to them, you will get yourself into a mess because that isn't what God's Word says or what many leaders under the headship of Jesus in the world today are teaching.

I don't know about you, but if I heard someone going against what our fathers today are teaching and what our forefathers—Abraham, Isaac and Jacob—taught, then I wouldn't follow them. I would choose, instead, to follow what God says in His Word.

✦ ✦ ✦

TITHING GOD'S WAY

*T*ithing and the giving of offerings are not an option for the child of God. If we desire to walk in His system of financial freedom then we must adhere to these two ordinances. They constitute God's divine law, which has been established to bless His children financially and materially. Remember that tithing is being faithful with what belongs to God, while giving offerings is being faithful with what belongs to us. Therefore, the more understanding we get concerning this divine plan of God the more we will enjoy our inheritance.

In the time of Malachi the prophet, the Israelites had strayed away from keeping some of the ordinances that their forefathers Abraham, Isaac and Jacob had kept. Then the Lord said that if they would return unto Him, that is, keep the ordinances again, then He would return unto them. Let's take a closer look at the words of his prophecy:

> **Even from the days of your fathers ye are gone away from mine ordinances, and have not kept them. Return unto me, and I will return unto you, saith the Lord of hosts. But ye said, Wherein shall we return?**

Will a man rob God? Yet ye have robbed me. But ye say, Wherein have we robbed thee? In tithes and offerings. Ye are cursed with a curse: for ye have robbed me, even this whole nation.

—MALACHI 3:7-9

In short, God was telling them that there were some things that He couldn't do for them unless they did what He told them to do. And what were the ordinances that God told them they needed to start keeping again? God answers this question in verse 8, saying essentially, "The bringing of their tithes and giving of their offerings." And what did God say He would do if they would return to Him by tithing and giving? He said, "I will return unto you." We already found out what that means back in the tenth chapter of this book when we looked at Proverbs 3:9-10. God said that if we would promote Him with tithes and offerings, then He would return to us blessings in our bank accounts, jobs and businesses!

Here in Malachi, however, God tells them that by withholding their tithes and offerings, they were robbing Him and opening the door for the curse of poverty to operate in their lives. This, of course, is just the opposite of God's reason for setting this law into motion. Clearly, then, if we don't keep these ordinances, then we won't be able to reap the benefits of them.

Where Should the Tithe Go?

✦ ✦ ✦

Where should the tithe go when it leaves our hands? Some folks believe that they can use the tithe however they want to as long as it is used for God's work. But if the tithe belongs to the Lord, then it doesn't belong to us. And if the tithe is God's property, then it isn't our property. If the tithe is holy and is God's, then we have absolutely no say as to where it belongs or what to do with it. It is God's, so we should only do what He says to do with it!

First of all, remember that under the new covenant, Jesus is our High Priest. Therefore, we would take the tithe to Him. Under the old covenant, God told the children of Israel to bring the tithe to Him. Further instruction revealed that when they brought their tithes to the sanctuary and the priest, they were in reality bringing them to God.

Now, if we are to bring our tithes to Jesus like they brought their tithes to God, then we would have to bring them to a physical place as they did, because Jesus isn't physically here to receive our tithes any more than God was there to receive theirs. So where should we take them?

The only physical place that we should go to under the new covenant that would compare to the physical place of the old covenant is the local church. Under the old covenant, the tabernacle was the house of God, but under the new covenant, the local church is the house of God, as you can clearly see in Paul's first letter to Timothy:

These things write I unto thee, hoping to come unto thee shortly: But if I tarry long, that thou mayest know how thou oughtest to behave thyself in the house of God, which is the church.

—1 TIMOTHY 3:14,15

The Greek word for *church* means "a calling out" and refers to a meeting, especially of a religious community.[1]

When we interpret this verse in context, we see that Paul is talking about the local church which has a pastor and helps ministers. Notice, Paul even said that we ought to know how to conduct, or behave, ourselves in the house of God, an actual physical location. (It is important to establish that point because I remember hearing one fellow say that the Bible calls us the house of God, therefore, we can tithe to ourselves! Now that is what I call ignorance gone to harvest!)

No, we can't tithe to ourselves any more than we can tithe to someone's house, but we *can* tithe to the local church, which is the house of God. This point is further established in Malachi.

> **Bring ye all the tithes into the storehouse, that there may be meat in mine house, and prove me now herewith, saith the Lord of hosts, if I will not open the windows of heaven, and pour you out a blessing, that there shall not be room enough to receive it.**
>
> —MALACHI 3:10

Notice that the words *storehouse* and *house* both refer to physical locations. And by reading the Old Testament, we know that the location referred to here is the tabernacle. That is where they brought their tithes to God. But today, under the new covenant, we bring our tithes to Jesus through the local church.

Bring All *of the Tithes*

✦ ✦ ✦

Notice that it says to bring *all* of the tithes into the storehouse. It doesn't say, "Split ye all the tithes." It says to bring them all to the same place! Some people bring part of the tithe, give part of the tithe, spend part of the tithe, send part of the tithe and designate part of the tithe until they reach the point that they have taken God right out of the picture. Listen, if the tithe is God's property—and it is—then it isn't ours! We don't have any right to spend, send, give or designate what is to be done with it. It is the Lord's, and it is holy unto the Lord, and we need to treat it as such!

Furthermore, this verse tells us that we are to tithe to one place *all of the time*. Notice that the word *tithes* is plural. That means tithing isn't a one-time occurrence. It is to be done continually because we continually receive income. And according to this verse, every time we tithe we are to bring it to the same place! We aren't to tithe in one place one time then in another place the next time. That is unscriptural!

"But, Brother Larry, I've been tithing to such-and-such a ministry, and someone told me that was okay." Someone may have told you it is okay, but that doesn't mean it is okay. You need to go by what God says in His Word, and He says to bring all of the tithes into the storehouse. The Hebrew word used here for *bring* means "to go or come."[2] It is referring to a person who is physically going somewhere. In other words, it is letting us know that we are to physically carry our tithes to a place that we go to regularly, that being the local church.

I realize that other ministries also provide good food to feed on just as the local church does, but they are not the house of God that is referred to in the Bible. They don't have the same type of "meat," or provision, that you and I need as believers.

For example, let's suppose that you have a child who has become deathly ill around two in the morning. Who are you going to call to come and pray and stand with you? Well, you won't call the nationally-known TV evangelist, because he won't come. You will call your pastor. And who are you going to call to do the funeral when you have had a death in the family? You aren't going to call the missionary in Timbuktu. You are going to call your pastor. And who are you going to call to perform the wedding of one of your children? You aren't going to call the radio preacher, because he won't come! No, you are going to call your pastor. If some loved one is in an accident and isn't expected to live through the night, who are you going to call? The well-known author of a Christian book won't be available, but do you know who will? You guessed it. Your pastor!

The tithe belongs in the local church so that provision, or "meat," is available for all the family members who are part of that local church. That includes nurseries, children's classrooms, youth facilities, carpet, chairs, sound systems and a whole lot more! And a substantial part of that provision means that the pastor is paid very well so that he doesn't have to work an outside job, nor be concerned about providing for his own personal needs and desires. Only then can he have the time necessary to provide what is needed in the lives of his sheep.

Windows-of-Heaven Blessings Promised

✦ ✦ ✦

When you look at the rest of this tenth verse, you will see what God will do when we tithe correctly. He says,

**...and prove me now herewith, saith the Lord
of hosts, if I will not open you the windows of
heaven, and pour you out a blessing, that there
shall not be room enough to receive it.**

The Hebrew word for *prove* is a lot stronger than what
comes across here. If we were to paraphrase in our own
language the definitions of this word, then God would
have said something like this: "Go ahead, check Me out,
investigate Me, try Me, put Me to the test and give Me an
opportunity to prove Myself to you!"[3]

In other words, God really means business here! He is
letting us know that He is ready to back up His words
concerning tithing. His promise is that He will open the
windows of heaven. The Hebrew word for *windows* could
refer to a "floodgate."[4] In fact, the same Hebrew word is
used in Genesis 7:11 where God flooded the earth in Noah's
day: **The windows of heaven were opened.**

When God opened the floodgates of heaven and poured
out rain, the creeks couldn't contain it, the streams couldn't
contain it, the rivers couldn't contain it, the lakes couldn't
contain it, the different oceans couldn't contain it and even the
mountains couldn't contain it. It was just too much to contain!

Do you know what comes out when the windows of
heaven are opened? Too much to contain! That is the God
we serve. He is the God of more than enough. He is the
God of too much, and He wants to open the floodgates of
financial blessings in our lives so that our cars can't
contain it, our closets can't contain it, our dressers can't
contain it, our pantries can't contain it, our homes can't
contain it, our wallets and purses can't contain it and our

banks can't contain it! God wants us to have more than enough. Now, that is worth shouting about!

But He doesn't stop there. Look at the next verse:

> **And I will rebuke the devourer for your sakes, and he shall not destroy the fruits of your ground; neither shall your vine cast her fruit before the time in the field, saith the Lord of hosts.**
>
> —MALACHI 3:11

Not only does God want to bless you, but He wants to protect you and all that you have.

Rebuke the Devourer

✦ ✦ ✦

Now let me share with you a truth that God revealed to me. First of all, let me ask you a question. Do you know people who have tithed for years and yet never received windows-of-heaven blessings? Sure you do! Why? Well, it sure isn't because God isn't doing His part. If He said that He would open the windows of heaven and pour out a blessing, then He will. So why aren't the blessings getting to the tithers? Because the blessings are being devoured before they get to them!

Notice the context in which this verse is set. God had told His children that when they weren't tithing, a curse would operate in their lives. Then He told them that if they would start tithing, He would rebuke the devourer. That tells me that it is the devourer who is operating and who is in charge of the curse.

140

In other words, just because we are redeemed from the curse of the law under the new covenant, that doesn't mean that the curse can't operate in our lives. First Peter 5:8-9 tells us, **Be sober, be vigilant; because your adversary the devil, as a roaring lion, walketh about, seeking whom he may devour: Whom resist steadfast in the faith.**

Notice that this verse lets us know that the devourer is the devil. He is out to steal, kill and destroy. Guess who this is written to? It is written to Christians. Why? Because the devil wants to devour your marriage, he wants to devour your job, he wants to devour your health, he wants to devour your finances and anything else that you will let him devour. And when those things happen in your life, they aren't the blessings of God. They are the curses of the devil.

"But, Brother Larry, I thought the devil was rebuked concerning my finances." He is, but that doesn't mean that we can just sit back and do nothing. We have to enforce the devil's defeat. James 4:7 says that we are to submit ourselves first of all to God, then we are to resist the devil, and he will flee. Ephesians 6:16 tells us that we can use the shield of faith to quench all the fiery darts of the wicked one who is trying to bring the curses into operation in our lives.

So it isn't that the devil hasn't been rebuked, because he has. As a matter of fact, he has been more than rebuked under the new covenant. The Hebrew word for *rebuke* means to "chide" or "reprove."[5] But under the new covenant, the devil has been more than just rebuked; he has been whipped, stripped and defeated!

Think about it for a minute. Concerning sin, the devil has been defeated, and yet he still brings that curse into the lives of Christians who let him. In other words, in order to stay free from sin, we have to exercise our faith and resist the temptations that come to us.

And what about sickness? Didn't Jesus take that curse upon Himself at Calvary according to 1 Peter 2:24? Yet there are many Christians suffering with that curse today.

Yes, the devil has been defeated concerning sin, sickness and poverty under the new covenant, yet Christians continue to be devoured in all these areas. Why? Because they aren't enforcing the devil's defeat, and he is wreaking havoc in their lives.

This is one of the main reasons that Christians haven't been receiving the windows-of-heaven blessings that are promised them. They have thought that they didn't have to do anything. But it is time to wake up, because the devil is going to try to devour your finances just as much as other blessings in your life (and sometimes even more). Don't let him do it!

When Jesus was tempted by the devil, what did He do? He said, "It is written." In other words, He spoke the Word! You should follow His example and do the same. When poverty or lack is trying to work in your life, stand up and say, "It is written. I am a tither; therefore, the windows of heaven are opening to me now and blessings are coming to me now. Satan, you have already been rebuked, and you can't devour my finances. You can't stop the blessings from coming to me through my job, business and investments, because that is what the Word calls the fruit of my ground. And you can't cause my car to break down on the road or steal any of my harvest, because

Malachi 3:11 says that my vine will not cast her fruit before its time in the field!"

When you take a bold stand based on what the Scriptures say about your finances, you not only quench every fiery dart of lack and poverty with your faith shield, but you also release all the blessings which Jesus has already provided to start pouring into your life. Furthermore, your actions will cause the devourer to seek elsewhere for whom he may devour because he found out that he couldn't devour you.

Don't Speak Out Stout Words
✦ ✦ ✦

Another reason why Christians who tithe haven't been receiving the blessings that are being poured out is found in Malachi 3:13, which says, **Your words have been stout against me, saith the Lord. Yet ye say, What have we spoken so much against thee?** Let's stop right there for a minute.

Notice that God said your words have been strong against Him. Now, if God said that you have spoken words that are against Him, then that means you have done it. There is no arguing about it. If He said you have, then you have. Malachi 3:14 goes on to specify what you have said either out loud or in your heart: **Ye have said, It is vain to serve God: and what profit is it that we have kept his ordinance?**

To make the meaning of this verse a little more clear, let me come up with a few paraphrases. See if you can relate with any of them:

"It has been useless to work with God by paying my tithes. How has it profited me when I have done my duty?"

"I've been tithing for years, and I'm not getting more than I can contain."

"I tried tithing, but it didn't work."

"I'm a tither, but it sure doesn't seem to be helping my finances."

"I don't understand why God doesn't bless me. I've been tithing."

All these statements, as well as other similar ones, God calls stout words against Him. They are saying just the opposite of what He just said in verses 10 and 11. Anything that you say contrary to those verses would be speaking against God. In fact, here is another statement that God got all over me about: "I can't afford to do that," or "I'll never be able to afford that."

Who said you won't ever be able to afford it? Did God? No! He said that if you are a tither He will open the windows of heaven and pour out blessings so that you can't contain them. That doesn't sound like you won't ever be able to afford it.

"But, Brother Larry, I can't deny the facts. The facts are the facts, and the fact is that I can't afford it!"

Did you notice that God said that your words are stout against Him? In other words, even though you may be speaking the facts, if the facts go against what God has said, then you are speaking against God! Facts, as we call them, are merely the world's way of defining the truth. In general, people think that the truth is whatever the circumstances around them dictate or what is perceived by the physical senses. However, when the facts go against God's Word, then you are not supposed to speak them.

You are to speak the TRUTH, and the truth is God's Word. (John 17:17.) When you do that, then the anointing, or power of God's Word, will change the facts!

That is what faith in God is all about. As believers, we are supposed to *believe* what God says. And if we truly believe in our hearts, then we will say what we believe with our mouths. That is what the Bible calls confession. It is how we use our tongues to release the power of life. (Prov. 18:21.) When you believe God's Word concerning your finances and then speak it out of your mouth, your faith releases the anointing that is upon God's Word, and that anointing will destroy the yokes of lack and poverty in your life!

Already the devil has convinced too many Christians not to talk about wealth and riches, telling them that if they do, then they will be coveting. Do you know why he doesn't want you to say anything about them? Because he knows that when you do that, your faith is released by the words that come out of your mouth. So he tries to get you to say what is contrary to God's Word or just to say nothing at all.

It is time that you as a believer get just as bold with your confession of God's Word in this area as you have been in other areas of your life. Doing so will cause you to move into a new realm of financial freedom and to walk in the great abundance that God wants you to have.

Speak the Word Over Your Tithes
✦ ✦ ✦

The mouth can stop the windows-of-heaven blessings, or it can cause them to flow right into your life. You have probably known people through the years who have tithed yet never received windows-of-heaven blessings. That is because all they did was drop the money in the container! That is only part of tithing or the giving of offerings.

When you take a look at Deuteronomy 26:1-11, you can see that God told the children of Israel to say something when they tithed. In verse 5, He tells them to *speak* of and *say* before the Lord how He has delivered them and blessed them and brought them into a place of prosperity, then thank Him from their hearts for it. The essence of what they were to say is found in verses 5-15, which, when paraphrased might read something like this:

"God, we were in a mess, but You have delivered us with Your mighty hand. You have brought us into a land that flows with prosperity. And now, we have obeyed You by tithing. We haven't eaten our tithe when things looked bad. We haven't used any portion of the tithe for anything that we weren't supposed to, and we haven't given it to any dead works. So, look down from heaven and bless us and all the things You have given us."

Why was God wanting them to speak these things? Because, according to Proverbs 18:21, the tongue has the ability to release words of life or words of death. And God wanted them to say what He says so that life would be working in their finances. Do you think that God has changed? Well, He hasn't. He still wants you to speak the Word to all areas of your life today. He wants you to speak life-filled words over your spirit, mind, emotions, will, body, marriage, children, job, finances and every other area you can think of! When you get your mouth involved in your tithing it activates the faith that you have in your heart and causes your sacrifice to be acceptable and well-pleasing to God.

When Jesus taught His disciples how to use the faith that God gave them, He said they would have to speak it out. (Mark 11:23,24 and Luke 17:5,6.) In other words, if you are just giving your tithe because the Word says to, but you aren't mixing any faith with it, then it isn't going to produce life in your finances.

So, when you bring your tithe, don't just drop it in and forget it! Speak over it what the Word says, declaring something like this:

"I am tithing to You, my Father God, and I thank You for bringing me out of bondage into blessings. Thank You for bringing me into a land of prosperity. I worship You and rejoice that I am free from poverty and lack. Thank You, God, for opening the floodgates of heaven and filling my bank accounts with abundance and blessing my job, businesses and investments. I am a tither and therefore, satan, you have no place in my finances. Take your hands off my money in Jesus' name! I commission the angels of heaven to bring me money, favor and things. I am blessed coming in and going out. I'm blessed in the city and in the country, and everything I put my hand to prospers. I call all my bills, loans and debt paid in full! I am a lender and not a borrower, because I have way too much! Glory to God!"

The bringing of our tithes or giving of our offerings incorporates the heart and mouth as well as the hand and checkbook or wallet. Instead of giving up on God's system of prosperity because it doesn't seem to be working for you, find out where you have been missing it and make the necessary corrections so that you can begin experiencing His wonderful provision for your financial freedom.

✦ ✦ ✦

THE LAW OF SEEDTIME AND HARVEST

*L*et me begin by quoting Mark 4:26-29:

> **And he said, So is the kingdom of God, as if a man should cast seed into the ground; And should sleep, and rise night and day, and the seed should spring and grow up, he knoweth not how. For the earth bringeth forth fruit of herself; first the blade, then the ear, after that the full corn in the ear. But when the fruit is brought forth, immediately he putteth in the sickle, because the harvest is come.**

Notice God says, "So is the kingdom of God," and then proceeds to tell us the principle, or law, by which it is governed. In other words, it is the very basis from which the kingdom of God operates. That means everything in God's kingdom operates within the framework of this passage of Scripture. It says that the kingdom of God operates by the law of *seedtime and harvest*. We are told in Genesis 8:22 that as long as the earth remains we will have seedtime and harvest. This is known as the *Law of Genesis*.

This law dictates that every seed produces after its own kind. In other words, if you plant peas, you get peas; if you plant oranges, you get oranges; and if you plant money, then you will get a financial harvest. God's entire kingdom operates according to this law. Whether it's in the spiritual, physical, financial or any other part of God's kingdom, if we want to reap a harvest, we must sow seed.

Since God's entire system operates on planting a seed and reaping a harvest, then what we plant—whether we plant the Word, our money, our time or our love—will determine what we reap. Therefore, when we sow finances into the work of God it is like a seed that is planted in the ground. Just as the earth brings forth fruit of herself so does God's kingdom. Our money sown into the Gospel will reap a financial harvest. But it doesn't come overnight any more than the natural seed will bring a full grown tree by the next day! Notice our verse says that after we plant the seed we go to bed and get up day after day and don't see anything happening initially, even though life is springing forth from the seed. Then when we do start seeing our seed produce, all we will see at first is just a little blade; then after a while we will see the ear and then sometime later the full corn in the ear. This is how God's system of finance works. We must plant seed if we want a harvest.

Someone may say, "Well, I just don't understand how God can bring me a financial harvest when I sow my money."

One thing that is really awesome about this divine financial law is that we don't have to know how God will bring our harvest to us. Did you notice verse 27 says, **he knoweth not how?** We don't have to know how; that is

God's part. Our part is to plant the seed and then just rest in faith as God's kingdom prepares our harvests! It brings forth fruit of itself just as the earth brings forth fruit of herself. Therefore, when we do our part we should expect God to do His part. That is what faith is all about and also what links us up to God's system. When we sow financial seeds into His kingdom, we will reap a financial harvest. Isn't that awesome? It's a wonderful place of peace and tranquility when you no longer have to worry about your money. It is freedom and liberty! It is called **the perfect law of liberty** (James 1:25).

Not a Get-Rich-Quick Scheme

✦ ✦ ✦

When you talk about a system of financial freedom that takes all the pressure off, this is it! No longer do we have to worry or enter into anxiety about our money. No longer do we have to be frustrated or allow strife to gain entrance into our financial matters. If we find ourselves running short, all we have to do is simply increase our giving to God.

"But Brother Larry, that just sounds like you're giving to get." Yes, in a sense, it does. But didn't you expect to *get* eternal life when you *gave* your life to Jesus? Did you know that you were operating the law of seedtime and harvest? When you planted your old life as a seed to God, then just as a natural seed has to die before life springs forth, you died and new life in Christ Jesus came forth. Well, what is the difference then? When we give money to promote the kingdom of God because we love Him and want to obey Him, then we should expect to receive a harvest from Him. That is what I call Bible faith, and it pleases our heavenly Father.

Unfortunately, some people get the wrong idea and think that I'm talking about a get-rich-quick scheme or magic formula. I'm not saying that you can put your money in this slot and pull this lever, then God will be like a big slot machine and make you rich. No, I'm not talking about formulas, pushing buttons, pulling levers, flipping switches or any such thing. What I'm talking about here is seeking first the kingdom of God by learning His system, then demonstrating our trust in Him by operating within it according to His Word.

Listen, God made the riches, He owns the riches, and He wants us to have riches in our lives. And He has designed His system to operate so simply that it confounds the wise. To the world it doesn't make any sense at all that you can become wealthy by giving large sums of money into God's kingdom. Yet, God's system works on the simple law of seedtime and harvest, otherwise known as giving and receiving, or sowing and reaping.

Our part then is to sow seeds of finances and material things in order to reap a harvest of wealth. Galatians 6:7 says, **Be not deceived; God is not mocked: for whatsoever a man soweth, that shall he also reap.** The Phillips translation reads, **...A man's harvest in life will depend entirely on what he sows.** It doesn't say our harvest depends on the will of God for our lives; neither does it say our harvest depends on the type of job we have. If we are not happy with our present financial harvests, then we need to begin a thorough examination of our sowing! We must understand that when we sow financial seeds into God's kingdom, we give God the legal right to take the wealth back out of the sinner's hands and put it into the hands of those to whom it belongs! Therefore, it is imperative that we study the rules that govern the law of seedtime and harvest so we can more easily partake of the benefits which it provides.

Sowing With Purpose

✦ ✦ ✦

One of the Scriptures that talks about this law is found in 2 Corinthians 9:7: **Every man according as he purposeth in his heart, so let him give; not grudgingly, or of necessity: for God loveth a cheerful giver.**

The Greek word for *purposeth* means "to choose for oneself before another thing (prefer)."[1] In other words, we not only have to make a decision once and for all to be givers, but we have to continually choose to give when opportunities arise, rather than use our money for something else. Of course we now understand that because we're putting God first, we will soon have plenty of harvest coming in so that we can do the other things we want to do at a later time.

The next portion of verse 7 indicates that there should be no reluctance or sense of compulsion on our part. **Let him give; not grudgingly, or of necessity.** In other words, don't let people twist your arm and force you to give and don't fall for some sob story that makes you feel like you have to give. ...**For God loveth a cheerful giver.**

153

The Amplified Bible states it this way:

> ...for God loves (He takes pleasure in, prizes above other things, and is unwilling to abandon or to do without) a cheerful (joyous, "prompt to do it") giver [whose heart is in his giving].

That is the heart of our Father God. He is a giver, and He wants us to be givers too!

Abound to Every Good Work
✦ ✦ ✦

And when we follow His example, He tells us in verse 8 exactly what He will do for us: **And God is able to make all grace abound toward you; that ye, always having all sufficiency in all things, may abound to every good work.**

I really like the Conybeare translation of this verse:

> **And God is able to give you an overflowing measure of all good gifts, that all your wants of every kind may be supplied at all times, and you may give of your abundance to every good work.**

And, of course, many people have heard *The Amplified* version of this verse, but it bears repetition:

> **And God is able to make all grace (every favor and earthly blessing) come to you in abundance, so that you may always and under all circumstances and whatever the need be self-sufficient [possessing enough to require no aid or support and furnished in abundance for every good work and charitable donation].**

Notice, God wants us to have an abundance of finances and wealth all the time so that no matter what situation we are facing or what circumstance we are in, we have so much money that we don't have to borrow from the bank to build the house, buy the car or do anything else we want to do. And we will have so much left over that every time we come in contact with a good work of the Gospel we are able to give to it in excess.

Now, friends, that is what I call rich! Actually, that is God's definition of rich. Not only are all of our needs, wants and desires supposed to be abundantly supplied, but we are to have so much left over that we can give ministries more than they need! Notice what that last phrase of verse 8 said again: ...**may abound to every good work.**

The Greek word for *abound* means "to superabound (in quantity or quality), be in excess, be superfluous; also (trans.) to cause to superabound or excel."[2] Now remember, this definition is in reference to our giving every time we come across a good work. That means we give them *more than enough,* or TOO MUCH! Perhaps you see a good ministry that is in need of $25,000 to complete a project that God told them to do, so you send them $30,000! Another ministry may need $10,000 right now to pay a radio bill, so you send them $15,000! That is what God is talking about in this verse! He wants us to give *in excess* to each and every good work! Well, in order to do that we are going to have to get the wealth into our hands.

Sowing Sparingly

✦ ✦ ✦

Now that we have looked at verses 7 and 8, let's back up to verse 6. Verses 7 and 8 have established that we are supposed to be regular and cheerful givers, which will result in God giving back to us in multiplied proportions. I like to say that verse 6 tells us how to get our financial harvests "flowing or slowing." Verse 6 says, **But this I say, He which soweth sparingly shall reap sparingly; and he which soweth bountifully shall reap also bountifully.**

The Greek word used for *sparingly* means "stingily."[3] In other words, a person who sows sparingly is stingy! I don't know about you, but I don't want God or people to refer to me as stingy. Just the sound of the word makes me want to get away from it! The paraphrase of this verse in *The Message* Bible uses those exact words: **Remember: A stingy planter gets a stingy crop.** Other paraphrases and translations word it just a little differently. *The Living Bible* says, **But remember this—if you give little, you will get little.** Another version says, **Remember this: The farmer who plants a few seeds will have a very small harvest.**[4] If I were going to paraphrase this verse I would say, "Just remember, if you give just a little, then all you are going to receive is just a little in return."

The latter part of Luke 6:38 makes a similar statement: **For with the same measure that ye mete withal it shall be measured to you again.** *The New Testament in Modern English* by J.B. Phillips says, **For whatever measure you use with other people, they will use in their dealings with you.** *The Modern Language Bible* by Berkeley reads, **For with the yardstick you use for measuring, you in turn shall be measured.** And finally, *The Living Bible* says, **Whatever measure you use to give—large or small—will be used to measure what is given back to you.**

In other words, if we give little we are going to get little. Our harvest in the financial realm as well as every other realm depends on what we sow, *period!* Let's look at another Scripture that will give us further insight. It is found in Proverbs 11:24. Quoting from *The Amplified Bible,* it reads, **There are those who [generously] scatter abroad, and yet increase more; there are those who withhold more than is fitting or what is justly due, but it tends only to want.**

I like to paraphrase the verse this way: "There are people who just keep giving their finances everywhere they turn and yet continue to grow richer. And there are also others who sow financial seed, but they hold back more than they should, only to find themselves facing more lack."

This tells us that there are people who scatter, or give, continually and yet, even though they are giving a lot away, they keep receiving larger harvests. That is the way God's financial system works! It is wonderful because not only are you blessing others by your giving, but also you are being blessed even more with greater harvests, which means your giving is going to keep increasing! That is essentially what Jesus meant when He said that it is *more of a blessing to give than to receive!* (Acts 20:35.)

But this verse also says that there are those who *withhold more than they should.* Instead of their sowing bringing them a good harvest it brings lack, deficiency and want in their lives. This verse says that they are giving, but indicates that they aren't giving in proportion to what they have. They are holding back more than they should, and it is actually working against them! When we hold back more than we should, that is what 1 Corinthians 9:6 refers to as sowing "sparingly." And when we withhold our seed, all we end up doing is delaying our harvest. As a matter of fact, if what you have right now is not big enough to be your harvest, then some of it must be your seed! Think about it. If you compare what you presently have to God's definition of *rich* in 2 Corinthians 9:8, then you will see very quickly that what you have is not all your harvest. That means it is time to start increasing your sowing. You have to get more seed in the ground if you want larger harvests!

It is possible that you may even be sitting on some of your seed. You may have it stored away in saving accounts and bank notes and only be receiving nominal returns. But if you would just get it invested into God's financial system, it would bring you much greater returns than your bank ever dreamed possible!

Now wait a minute. I didn't say savings accounts and bank notes are wrong. Obviously, we need bank accounts because God says He will bless our storehouses and fill them with plenty! But what I did say was that if you are trying to hold on to what you have and, in the process, are withholding more than you should, then it isn't going to bring you abundance. Oh, you may be getting a little interest here and there, but, compared to God's system, what you are receiving is like a grain of sand at the beach. Don't settle for a grain when God wants to give you the whole beach!

Led by God or Circumstance?
✦ ✦ ✦

Why would people withhold more than they should or refrain from giving, when God has promised multiplied blessings in return? The main reason that I have seen is that they haven't yet learned to trust God in this area of their lives. They are basing their financial decisions on their natural circumstances and trying to figure everything out on their own.

Proverbs 3:5-6 tells us not to depend on our own understanding, but to put God first in everything we do so that He can direct our paths. In other words, we can't rely on our own intellect if we are going to trust God. It's a heart matter, not a head matter!

It is directly after these verses that verses 9 and 10 follow, telling us that if we will honor the Lord with our tithe, the firstfruits of our increase and give offerings of our substance because we trust, or have faith in, God, then He will fill our bank accounts with plenty.

Look with me at Ecclesiastes 11:3 because it gives further insight into why people don't give like they should: **If the clouds be full of rain, they empty themselves upon the earth: and if the tree fall toward the south, or toward the north, in the place where the tree falleth, there shall it be.**

Now, this isn't some deep, hidden revelation. Look closely at what it says. If the clouds become full of rain, it is going to rain. And if a tree falls to the north or the south, then that is where it is going to be! Why is God being so simplistic here? Because He is leading up to verse 4: **He that observeth the wind shall not sow; and he that regardeth the clouds shall not reap.**

In other words, your present situation may look just like a tree that has been blown over by the wind and is not going anywhere. And your circumstances may look dark and cloudy like there is nothing but rain and storms ahead. But don't focus your attention on everything going on around you, because then you will neither sow nor reap a harvest! Both the wind and clouds are a part of the world's system. They are elements that you have to deal with on a daily basis. They try to bring fear and confusion into your life to hinder you from receiving the blessings of heaven. Fear is probably the number one hindrance to people's tithing and giving. They fear that they will not have enough if they tithe or give. In essence, they have observed the wind and regarded the clouds. In other words, they have not put their trust in God.

But what does faith do and how does it act? If we were to take the reciprocal of this verse, I believe it clearly shows the path of faith: "He who doesn't focus his attention on his circumstances, nor fix his eyes on the world's economy, will surely sow his seed and reap all of his harvest too!"

God wants us to tithe and give our way into financial wealth! That keeps Him as Lord of our money, keeps our eyes off our money and on Him and keeps us in a position of peace and rest. It is *truly* the best system of financial freedom available on the earth today, BAR NONE!

All the Scriptures we have looked at in this chapter have revealed to us that we determine how big our harvest is going to be by our giving. They have also shown us that none of God's children are excluded from operating within this divine system—God is no respecter of persons! But most of us, at one time or another, have fallen into THE TRAP.

✦ ✦ ✦

WORKING FOR A LIVING—IT'S A TRAP

*D*id you know that nowhere in the Bible does it tell you to work for a living? Second Thessalonians 3:10 tells us that if we don't work then we shouldn't eat. First Timothy 5:8 says that if we don't provide for our families then we are worse than an unbeliever. Other Scriptures show us men of God working jobs that provided income to take care of immediate needs, but nowhere does it say that our living, or how we live financially, is determined by our jobs. In fact, on the contrary, all of the Scriptures that we have already looked at have said no such thing!

Think about it for a moment. If our jobs were God's way of bringing us the abundance of riches that He talks about in His Word, then His way would be a respecter of persons. Why? Because a school janitor could not make as much as a lawyer could make. Neither could a mechanic make as much as a surgeon. There are many companies with people who have been promoted to the highest paid positions of those companies, and yet they still fall way short of financial freedom. There are many different vocations where you could never work long enough or hard enough to earn wages that would bring you that kind of wealth. It is known that some people are called by God to be certain things, such as school teachers, their entire lives. That would mean that they could not make as big a living as the superintendent. If that is how God's system worked, then He would be a respecter of persons and simply not fair! In that case, only the people with the top paying positions would have a chance to become financially free. Besides that, if everyone were the company president, then none of them would have any help!

Working for a living is not God's system of prosperity; it is the world's system of prosperity. And yet many of us have worked for a living most of our lives. The thinking is that if you can just get enough education so that you can get the right job, and work there long enough, and get enough raises and bonuses, and get enough money saved up, then maybe you can live comfortably and even retire without too many financial worries. This system is what has caused people to have to work more than one job. It has put children at the disadvantage of not being raised by their parents because both parents have to work to make ends meet. And unfortunately it is even what has caused many Christians to miss the will of God for their lives, because they accepted jobs based on the pay, and they don't even enjoy the job!

Friends, that is not God's way to financial freedom! His way is *much higher* than that. Therefore, He must have a system established whereby all people, from all walks of life, working all types of jobs can become financially free. His system must be able to bless the school teacher as well as the principal, the cashier as well as the store owner, the farmer as well as the land developer and the church janitor as well as the pastor. And guess what? He does! His system is called seedtime and harvest, sowing and reaping, giving and receiving. The way for God's children to become wealthy is by operating according to God's law of increase.

"Okay, Brother Larry, then if I don't have to work for a living, why should I work?"

Well, first of all, the books of 2 Thessalonians and 1 Timothy make it clear that we are supposed to work. But let's get further understanding concerning our work from Ephesians 4:28:

> **Let him that stole steal no more: but rather let him labour, working with his hands the thing which is good, that he may have to give to him that needeth.**

This verse implies that if we are not working then we are stealing. In other words, if we are not using our hands to make money, then more than likely we are mooching off of others to get by. That is not what God calls living by faith; on the contrary, He calls it stealing! *The Living Bible* reads, **If anyone is stealing he must stop it and begin using those hands of his for honest work so he can give to others in need.**

Yes, this lets us know that we are supposed to work! Did you notice, in the *King James Version,* the two words *labour* and *working?* The first one means "to feel fatigue; by impl. to work hard."[1] The second one means "to toil (as a task, occupation, etc.)."[2] So we are supposed to work, and this verse even gives some guidelines about the type of work we can do: ...**working with his hands the thing**

which is good. Notice, the two different translations say that we are supposed to work *honest* and *good* professions.

That would eliminate some jobs! If we are supposed to work honest jobs then we couldn't have jobs that require us to lie, cheat or take advantage of people. If we are supposed to have vocations that are good, then we couldn't be drug pushers, thieves, strip dancers, gamblers or anything else that would go against God's Word. This verse tells us that we are supposed to use our hands to work good jobs.

I'm going to say something else here that may be difficult for some people to hear, but I trust that you will believe the Word nonetheless. Any job that continually takes you away from attending and being involved in church *is not good!* That goes against what God's Word says. We are told in Hebrews 10:21-25 not to forsake coming together as a body so we can draw near to Jesus. And God says that we are supposed to do it even more as we see the return of Jesus getting closer. So if our jobs, businesses or vocations are not allowing us to be intricately involved in our churches, then we need to make the necessary adjustments or prayerfully consider what else God has for us. Our lives should revolve around the church and its activities. So if you don't have a church that is exciting and full of life, then change churches. It has been said, "A church alive is worth the drive!"

I'm going to say it again: Any job, business or trade that takes us away from church and the church family is not good.

Okay, now we know that God wants us to work, and that He wants us to work good and honest jobs, but what is the main reason for our working? Look again at the verse: ...**let him labour, working with his hands the thing which is good, that he may have to give.**

Does this verse say that we are supposed to work so that we can make a living? No, it says we are supposed to work so that we have finances to give. In other words, we are not supposed to be working for a living; we are supposed to be "working for a giving" and then letting our giving determine our living!

Our harvest depends on our giving, not on the type of job we have; and our harvest is what God wants us to live on and give from! Our jobs and businesses are supposed to provide seed for us to sow. Then as we sow bountifully, we will reap bountifully and have abundance from which to live.

Second Corinthians 13:1 says, **In the mouth of two or three witnesses shall every word be established.** So let's look at three Scriptures that will establish this truth that our living, or the harvest that we live from, is not determined by our vocation.

The first Scripture is found in 2 Corinthians 9:6 and reads, **But this I say, He which soweth sparingly shall reap sparingly; and he which soweth bountifully shall reap also bountifully.**

Does this verse say that he who gets the better job shall reap bountifully? No! In fact this verse says nothing at all about the kind of job we have with regard to our harvest. It simply says that if we want to reap bountifully, or have large financial harvests come to us, then we have to give bountifully. Therefore, the size of our harvests will depend on how much seed we sow.

The next Scripture is found in Luke 6:38 and reads, **Give, and it shall be given unto you; good measure, pressed down, and shaken together, and running over, shall men give into your bosom. For with the same measure that ye mete withal it shall be measured to you again.**

Some people try to convince others that this verse is not referring to giving money or material things, but if you read it in context you will be able to see that these are included. The previous verses talk about loving, lending, being merciful, forgiving, not judging and not condemning. Then verse 38 talks about giving! Not giving love, mercy or any of those other things. We know those things operate by seedtime and harvest as well, but those are already dealt with in verses 35-37. Verse 38 talks about giving as in sowing financial and material seed.

Notice what it says: **Give, and it shall be given unto you.** Remember, the whole kingdom operates on this principle. Plant, and you shall reap a harvest; give, and it shall be given unto you. Then the verse tells us the result of our giving: **It shall be given unto you; good measure, pressed down, and shaken together, and running over.** In other words, God multiplies your seed sown. (See 2 Corinthians 9:10.)

Does that mean our harvest is just going to drop out of the sky? No, God tells us in this verse the primary way that He will bring our harvests to us: **...shall men give into your bosom.**

Whom does this say God uses to bring your harvest to you? He uses men! God can influence people to bless you even more than the devil can influence people to curse you! When we give, it allows the Holy Ghost and our angels to begin influencing people to show us favor and to give us money and things. However, this does not apply to stingy givers. We have to remember that the harvest we get depends on our planting: **For with the same measure that ye mete withal it shall be measured to you again.**

For clarity's sake here are some other translations: *The New Testament in Modern English* by Phillips says, **For whatever measure you use with other people, they will use in their dealings with you.** *The Modern Language Bible* by Berkeley reads, **For with the yardstick you use for measuring, you in turn shall be measured.** And *The Living Bible* says, **Whatever measure you use to give—large or small—will be used to measure what is given back to you.**

Did you notice that this verse doesn't say that if you get the good job, then it will be given back to you? No, once again, the harvest that God wants us to live from is not based on our job status. Our harvest depends on what we sow, period!

Our third Scripture is found in Proverbs 11:24-25:

There is that scattereth, and yet increaseth; and there is that withholdeth more than is meet, but it tendeth to poverty. The liberal soul shall be made fat: and he that watereth shall be watered also himself.

The New International Version reads: **One man gives freely, yet gains even more; another withholds unduly, but comes to poverty. A generous man will prosper; he who refreshes others will himself be refreshed.**

Does this verse say that the man who gets the better job will gain even more? Does it say that only the president of the company will prosper? Does it say that people will only give to and refresh you if you are well known? No, it says that the one who gives freely, who is generous and who blesses others, will be the one who gains riches, prospers and is blessed by others.

Now let's go back to our original Scripture found in Ephesians 4:28. It tells us to work a good, honest job **...that he may have to give.** No longer do we have to work for a living! Someone shout, Hallelujah! From now on we will "work for a giving" and then let our giving determine our living!

The exciting part about this is that it will work regardless of the type of job you have or what kind of business you own. It will work whether you are the "top dog on the totem pole" or at the "bottom of the ladder." In other words, the church janitor can be richer than the pastor if he outgives him. Why? Because his living is not determined by the paycheck he receives from his job; it is determined by his giving. Folks, it just boils down to this: The more seed that we sow, the bigger our harvests will be!

Can you imagine what Christians will do when they get the revelation of this? They will be working overtime so they have more seed to sow! They will be looking for ways to make money so they can give more to God, which in turn will cause their living to be increased! Glory to God!

This will free Christians up to find the jobs that they truly enjoy and the jobs that God wants them to have, regardless of the income. No longer will their source be their jobs but it will be God. Christians will no longer be moving from here to there because of their job situations, but they will be moving because God tells them He wants them to be involved in a particular church or ministry!

There are so many Christians who are working jobs that are literally robbing them of God's best. They don't have time for their families or their churches, and they wonder why their relationship with God, their marriages and their families are falling apart.

It is time for us to wake up! Let's start pursuing God's plan and seek first the kingdom of God, then God will begin adding and multiplying all the rest unto us. That means our jobs, homes, cars, clothing and everything else will be blessed!

Now, if this is all wonderfully new revelation to you and you are presently in a job that you feel is not the right one, please don't go quit your job tomorrow. You didn't get yourself into this mess overnight, and you aren't going to get out of it overnight, either. But, if you'll start seeking God in prayer, being faithful in church and being a tither and a giver, God will change things for the better—and more quickly than you could have ever dreamed of!

Since God's financial system is no respecter of persons, then everybody in the body of Christ can become financially free. Just quit looking to your job as the source of your harvest, and start looking to your job as the source of some seed. Notice, I didn't say they are the sources of *all* your seed. Why? Because 2 Corinthians 9:10 tells us that God gives seed to the sower: **Now he that minis-tereth seed to the sower both minister bread for your**

food, and multiply your seed sown, and increase the fruits of your righteousness.

This tells us that God will give us seed just for the purpose of sowing. Sometimes God will give you a financial blessing just for you to give it all away! But to whom does this verse say God gives seed? The sower! Not the one who wants to sow or who is believing to sow, but the one who is actually doing it! I've heard people say things like "Now, if you don't have anything to give, just hold up your hand and see it full by faith," or "Believe God for some seed to sow." But notice that the verse says God gives seed to the *sower!* If you are not a sower, you don't qualify! And, contrary to what you may have heard, everyone has something to sow. It doesn't matter if you are the poorest person in the world, you still have something to sow. That is why I made the statement "You have to start where you are; then God can take you where He wants you to be."

Where Do We Give?
✦ ✦ ✦

Now we know that we are supposed to be givers who plant seed continually and that we are not supposed to be stingy in our giving. So then, where does the Bible instruct us to plant our seed? Part of the answer to that question is found in this same verse, Ephesians 4:28. It already told us to work with our hands at good jobs so that we can have money to give. But, give where? ...**Let him labour, working with his hands the thing which is good, that he may have to give to him that needeth.**

God says we are supposed to give to *him that needeth.*

For years I always thought that this verse and others that talk about helping those in *need* meant giving to the poor. Of course I realize that poor people definitely have needs. Our society even refers to them as "the needy." However, rich people, as well as people who are neither rich nor poor, also have needs. So, the teaching that follows will expand our thinking about what God means in this verse and other verses when referring to the word *need.*

Before we discuss this word, let me ask you some questions. In light of what you have already learned in this book, do you think that God just wants to give you enough to get by? Do you think that He is interested in nothing more than just giving you the bare necessities of life? Is He the Lord your shepherd and so you are full of want?

On the other hand, do you think that God could use someone to plant some seed into your life toward something that you desire? Do you think He wants you to have more than enough? Do you think that He is a God who can give you the desires of your heart?

I am stirring up your minds to remember all the things that we have already learned from the Word of God. Things like these: God owns all the wealth; He is an excessive giver; we are His children, and He likes giving to us; Jesus became poor so we could be rich; God wants us to live wealthy and then leave our wealth to our grandkids when we die; God said we could reap bountifully and that He would fill our bank accounts with plenty; and if we serve and obey Him we will spend our days in prosperity and our years in pleasures.

I have reminded you of those things so that I could say this: God will meet your needs, wants and desires no matter what level of prosperity you are at right now. And He can use people who are "working for a giving" to sow into your life and help you fulfill all kinds of financial dreams. What I am saying is that every one of us could fall into the category of *him that needeth.*

Now, with that understanding, let's take a look at this word *needeth* here in Ephesians 4:28. It comes from a Greek word which means "employment, i.e. an affair; also (by impl.) occasion, demand, requirement or destitution:—business, lack, necessary, need, use, want."[3]

We can quickly understand by looking at these definitions that the word *needeth* refers to a lot of different situations that people will face. *Him that needeth* could have to do with your employment or business. It may have to do with an occasion or maybe the local building codes demanding or requiring something that takes a lot of money. It could be something you need or could use, but it may be something you just want! All of these situations, and many others, fall into the category of *him that needeth.*

We see this same Greek word used in other places in the New Testament as well. Let's look at some of them. Do you remember the passage of Scripture that we looked at in our third chapter, in which Jesus told the disciples to go get Him a colt to ride? Jesus said out of His own mouth, *...the Lord hath **need** of him.* (Mark 11:3.) The word *need* used there is the same word used here in Ephesians. Well, remember, we already discussed the fact that Jesus didn't *need* the donkey because He was poor. Actually, the need was to fulfill Scripture, and the word *requirement* is one of the definitions of this word *need*. Well, everyone who is a tither and giver has a *need,* or *requirement,* to fulfill Scripture, that being to have their bank accounts filled with plenty, and only God can meet that requirement!

Another place where we find this same Greek word for *need* being used is in Philippians 4:19, where Paul says that God will supply all our *need*. Well, again we know that God not only wants to supply our needs, but He wants to give us exceeding, abundantly above all that we can ask or think! (See Ephesians 3:20.) Then that means that God will use people who are "working for a giving" to sow into our lives to meet financial wants and desires.

One other place where Paul used this same word for *need* is found in Philippians 2:25, in which he refers to Epaphroditus as one who **ministered to my wants.** Epaphroditus didn't just minister to Paul's needs; he attended to things that Paul wanted as well!

So let's look again at some of the definitions of the word *needeth*. It means employment, occasion, demand, requirement, business, lack, necessary, need, use, want. With these definitions in mind, "giving to *him that needeth*" could embrace a variety of situations that would dictate where we could sow seed. It might include someone who has an occasion to go on an overseas trip and so you give seed to help them. It might also include your pastor, church and other ministries who are busy doing the work of God. The more you do for God, the more money it takes. Traveling, television, radio, books, magazines, recording albums, building larger facilities for churches and ministries, equipment...

The list goes on and on. This is all part of getting the Gospel out, and it takes lots of money to do all those things!

God has called men and women to do mighty works for Him in these last days, and He has placed large visions inside them. Each step that they take in fulfilling their visions has needs associated with it. *The bigger the vision, the bigger the need.* In other words, vision creates need. Let me give you an illustration. A pastor may start out by having church services in a small auditorium. As he fills it up, God expands his vision to reach more people. So he goes on the radio and starts teaching, which draws more people to the church. He then has to plan to move into a larger facility. God then leads him to go on television, and before long he has outgrown his facility again! That is what I mean when I say the bigger the vision, the bigger the need.

The Laborer Is Worthy of His Reward

❖ ❖ ❖

While the pastors and ministers of the Gospel are out fulfilling God's vision, the rest of the body of Christ is supposed to be giving to them so that all of their needs, wants and desires are abundantly provided for and so they don't have to work at secular jobs in order to get by. When a pastor is divided between the ministry and a secular job, it is more difficult for him to fulfill his responsibilities the way God had intended for him to. God is the One who set up this system. Look at 1 Corinthians 9:14: **Even so hath the Lord ordained** (commanded) **that they which preach the gospel should live of the gospel.** We can see this principle at work in Acts 6:2-4:

Then the twelve called the multitude of the disciples unto them, and said, It is not reason that we should leave the word of God, and serve tables. Wherefore, brethren, look ye out among you seven men of honest report, full of the Holy Ghost and wisdom, whom we may appoint over this business. But we will give ourselves continually to prayer, and to the ministry of the word.

Notice, Paul calls the ministry a "business." (By the way, this word *business* is also the same Greek word used for *needeth* in Ephesians 4:28, showing us that ministers qualify as *him that needeth*.) A minister's primary responsibility (his business) is to spend time in prayer, study the Word and then minister to people as God directs.

If we as Christians are doing our spiritual duty, then our pastors and other ministers who feed us the good Word of God should not be tied down to jobs that are taking precious hours each day away from their callings. Neither should they be concerned about not having enough money from their salaries to provide for their needs and wants. This can only happen when we receive understanding of how God's system works and abide by its rules. It is our responsibility as Christians to provide, and provide well, for our ministers.

First Timothy 5:17-18 further elaborates on this truth:

Let the elders that rule well be counted worthy of double honour, especially they who labour in the word and doctrine. For the scripture saith, Thou shalt not muzzle the ox that treadeth out the corn. And, **The labourer is worthy of his reward.**

Verse 18 starts out with the words **For the scripture saith.** That is letting us know that what is said in verse 17 is based on the Scriptures quoted in verse 18. Let's look at the two Scriptures that are quoted.

The first Scripture, **Thou shalt not muzzle the ox that treadeth out the corn,** is a reference from Deuteronomy 25:4 and is also found in Paul's writings to the Corinthian church in 1 Corinthians 9:9. It simply means that if you are using animals to plow your fields, pull your wagons or do any other work, then make sure you take good care of them. Make sure they are watered, fed and well rested. Why? Because their wellbeing will affect their productivity, which will directly affect your harvest!

Let's read what Paul says in 1 Corinthians 9:9-11. The *New International Version* reads:

> **For it is written in the Law of Moses: "Do not muzzle an ox while it is treading out the grain." Is it about oxen that God is concerned? Surely he says this for us, doesn't he? Yes, this was written for us, because when the plowman plows and the thresher threshes, they ought to do so in the hope of sharing in the harvest. If we have sown spiritual seed among you, is it too much if we reap a material harvest from you?**

We can clearly see that when Paul uses oxen here, it is an analogy for us to understand that we are supposed to financially take care of our pastors and other ministers of the Gospel. And just like taking good care of the oxen would affect our harvest, so too will the way we take care of our ministers. Remember, we are operating under the law of seedtime and harvest.

Now, notice something else that Paul says: **If we have sown spiritual seed among you, is it too much if we reap a material harvest from you?**

When Paul says *we,* he is talking about himself, the pastor and the other people with fivefold ministry gifts, such as the prophets, teachers and evangelists, who have visited the church and taught them the Word of God. So when Paul uses oxen as an example, he is referring to the other ministry gifts as well as the pastor. With that in mind, let's go back to 1 Timothy 5:18 and look at the second Scripture that Paul quoted: **The labourer is worthy of his reward.**

Jesus uses this statement when He is talking to His twelve disciples and also when He is sending out the seventy disciples. (Matt. 10:10; Luke 10:7.) In these Scriptures He refers to ministers as laborers and workman. The term *labourer* in the Greek means to "toil" as in an "occupation."[4] The Greek word for *hire* means "pay for service" and speaks of a "reward" or "wages."[5] In other words, Jesus is indicating that men and women who are called of God into the ministry are to be paid for their services. Did you notice that He calls the ministry an occupation? He is letting us know that the minister's pay ought to be based on business standards. What does that mean? In other words, when a man goes to work for a company, he doesn't get the same pay as the president. He has to prove himself faithful, have a good work ethic and have longevity with the company before he qualifies for top pay. You can see that this standard applies to ministers as well by going back to our text in 1 Timothy 5. Verse 17 says, **Let the elders that rule well be counted worthy of double honour, especially they who labour in the word and doctrine.** The Greek word for *elder* here means "senior" but goes beyond just referring to age, because in this same letter, in chapter 3, Paul says that a minister is not supposed to be put in a position of leadership as a *novice.* In other words, just because someone is older doesn't make him an elder in God's ranks. Putting this verse in modern language, you could say, "Let the seasoned ministers who rule well...."

What does it mean to rule well? The Greek word for *rule* means "to stand before, i.e. (in rank) to preside, or (by impl.) to practise:—maintain, be over, rule."[6] This lets us know that there is order and structure in God's kingdom and that His ministers are placed in positions of rank and leadership. *Strong's Concordance* tells us that the word *well* usually refers to someone who is ruling "morally" and "honestly."[7] Vine's says that this Greek word "is usually translated 'well,' indicating what is done rightly."[8] So the minister who is referred to here is one who is a person of integrity and has the highest standards with regard to his conduct. (Paul goes into more detail about these when discussing the attributes of a minister in 1 Timothy 3.)

So, how much should seasoned ministers who are doing their jobs well receive? Verse 17 says, **Let the elders that rule well be counted worthy of double honour.**

It says we are supposed to *count them worthy.* That means "to think meet, fit, right; to judge worthy, deem deserving."[9] That means our thinking should be that they are entitled to, or deserving, of something. And just what is it that they are entitled to and deserving of? The verse says **...of double honour.**

The Greek word *honour* means "a value, i.e. money paid."[10] In other words, our thinking should be that we expect our seasoned ministers of the Gospel to get paid double the amount or twice as much as they would if they were the president or C.E.O. of a secular company! After all, they are in the top ranks of God's company! And our verse goes on to say, **...especially they who labour in the word and doctrine.**

You can always tell when a minister has labored in the Word of God and in preparation for delivering what God has given him, because hearing it will always lift you up, encourage you to be a better Christian and push you forward in the kingdom of God. And, according to God, that kind of notable preacher is due double the wages. Unfortunately, some are still of the opinion that preachers shouldn't get paid much, even if they are seasoned ministers of God's Word.

What those people don't understand is that God has placed these ministers as leaders of His people and they are important to us as Christians. They watch over our souls (Heb. 13:17), feed us (1 Pet. 5:2), take care of us (1 Tim. 3:5) and become examples for us to pattern our lives after (1 Pet. 5:3, 1 Tim. 3:12). Plus, they do a whole lot more than what you will ever know or hear about. Therefore, your pastor and other ministers who help you in your Christian walk are worthy of top pay. They should be among the first who come to mind when we are giving *to him that needeth!* If every one of us will do our share in giving to the men and women of God who sow into our lives, then they will be abundantly provided for, and we will continue to enjoy greater harvests.

Besides that, when we give to them and sow toward the needs and desires of their lives and ministries, we are also demonstrating the love of God in our own lives! First John 3:16-17 says, **Hereby perceive we the love of God, because he laid down his life for us: and we ought to lay down our lives for the brethren. But whoso hath this world's good, and seeth his brother have need, and shutteth up his bowels of compassion from him, how dwelleth the love of God in him?**

Notice that giving is connected with our displaying the love of God in our lives. In essence, this is saying that our giving is our proof that we love God! A closer look at the verse reveals to us *what* we are supposed to give, as well as *to whom* we are supposed to give. Verse 17 starts out by saying, **But whoso hath this world's good....**

The Greek word for *good* means "that by which life is sustained, resources, wealth, goods."[11] In other words, it is referring to the money and things that you have in this world. That is your livelihood, and that is what you are supposed to give. Now, to whom are we supposed to give? The verse continues, **...and seeth his brother have need....**

The Greek word used for *brother* is a connective participle used both literally and figuratively.[12] That simply means that you can be a brother by birth into the same natural family, or you can be a brother as in the family of God. Out of the 320 times this word is used in the New

Testament, by far the majority refer to *brother* as in the body of Christ. So I believe that this verse is talking about giving to our brothers in the Lord. And it says we are supposed to give to them if we see that they have a *need*.

The word *need* in this verse is the same word used in Ephesians 4:28, where we saw that we are supposed to be "working for a giving" so that we will have to *give to him that needeth.* Remember, it means need, want, use, require and a whole lot more! So when this verse in 1 John says that if we see our *brother have need,* then we know it entails not only a family with no food in the cupboards, but a whole lot more.

Maybe your pastor needs or wants a new car. Well, if you have the resources and wealth to buy him one, then go get him the one he wants. If you see another minister with a *need* in his personal life or ministry and you have the means to meet it, then do it! I'm telling you, or better yet, God is telling you, that you will be blessed abundantly for it! Furthermore, it will show God and others how much His love is working in you. There is a saying, "The proof of the puddin' is in the eatin'." Well, in this case, the proof of your lovin' is in your givin'!

Continually be looking for ministers and ministries to give to. If they are good ground and they have been a blessing to you or your church, then be a blessing to them. And don't withhold more than you should. Listen, if you are concerned about missing God, make sure that you miss Him by giving too much and not by giving less than you should. It is a win-win proposition!

This is a part of the Bible that has been rarely preached, and yet it is a very important part of God's Word.

✦ ✦ ✦

DIVINE OPPORTUNITIES

*N*ow that we have learned how important our giving is in order to establish financial freedom in our lives, let's talk about where the main opportunities will present themselves for us to sow for future harvests. We will begin by reading some instructions that Paul gave to the church at Galatia. They are found in Galatians 6:6-10:

> Let him that is taught in the word communi-
> cate unto him that teacheth in all good things. Be
> not deceived; God is not mocked: for whatsoever
> a man soweth, that shall he also reap. For he that
> soweth to his flesh shall of the flesh reap corrup-
> tion; but he that soweth to the Spirit shall of the
> Spirit reap life everlasting. And let us not be
> weary in well doing: for in due season we shall
> reap, if we faint not. As we have therefore oppor-
> tunity, let us do good unto all men, especially
> unto them who are of the household of faith.

This passage of Scripture gives us some insight as to where we can continually plant seed and put ourselves in the best position to reap a continual harvest in our lives.

Let's examine it closely to further our understanding. It starts with **Let him that is taught in the word.**

This applies to every one of us who is taught the Word of God. And the foremost place that we are taught the Word of God should be our local churches, because most of us are attending our churches two or more times every week and being fed each time we go. This verse also indicates that we should be learning and growing in the knowledge of God's Word wherever we attend church.

We are then instructed as to what we are supposed to do after we are taught the Word: **Let him that is taught in the word communicate unto him that teacheth.** Notice, it says we are supposed to *communicate* to the one who has taught us the Word. The Greek word for *communicate* means "to come into communion or fellowship with, to become a sharer, be made a partner."[1] *Strong's Concordance* says it means to "share" or to "distribute." In other words, in its simplest terms, it means to give. Listen to how some of the other translations and paraphrases word this verse. *The New Testament in Modern English* by J.B. Phillips says, **...contribute toward the livelihood of his teacher.** *The Amplified Bible* reads, **...share all good things with his teacher [contributing to his support].** *The New English Bible* states, **...give his teacher a share of all good things he has.** Moffatt's Translation declares, **...must share all the blessings of life with those who teach them the Word.** *The Living Bible* announces, **Those who are taught the Word of God should help their teachers by paying them.**

This verse is showing us that we have an obligation to give offerings to ministers who teach us the Word. And, according to this verse, we are supposed to give to them every time they work and feed us the good Word of God! It doesn't say we are supposed to give to them every once in a while. It says we are supposed to give to them when we are taught the Word. In essence, that would be like saying, "Let him who eats in the restaurant pay for his food." Well, does that mean that you could go eat at the restaurant three times but only pay once? No, you would pay for the food each time you ate at the restaurant.

That explains why most churches, when they have a guest minister in the church, receive a love offering each time the minister preaches. What they are doing is giving the people who have been taught the Word an opportunity to bless the minister, as well as sow seed for their own harvests. Did you notice the verse says, **Let *him?*** It doesn't say, "Let them" or "Let the church"; it says let *him.* That means the individual who has been taught the Word. This verse shows us that the giving of an honorarium is unscriptural! What I mean by *honorarium* is when a pastor does not give the people a chance to give into the minister's life, but instead just gives him a certain amount. Of course there is nothing wrong with a church as a body giving an offering out of the church account to bless the minister because they have been taught the Word. In fact, they will be blessed if they do. But this verse is talking to individuals who are sitting in the services and being taught the Word of God. If they are not given an opportunity to give into that minister's life after they have been taught the Word, then they are being robbed of a chance to obey the Word, bless the minister and sow for their own future harvests!

Many pastors have a revelation of this, so they don't worry that the people's offerings are going to take away from the church's finances. They know that in reality they are going to help the individuals, which in turn will bless the church financially. And after many years of observation we have readily seen that these churches are not struggling financially at all, but are being abundantly blessed!

I have been to places where the minister finished preaching and yet no love offering was received; however, I observed people giving that minister money and material things because they had been taught the Word of God. Now, those people have a revelation of this verse!

Remember, in 1 Corinthians 9:11, that Paul admonished us to give of our material wealth to the minister who has fed our spirits and renewed our minds with the Word of God. And remember also that God looks at the ministry as a business and that the laborer, or worker, is worthy of his pay. Well, does a businessman work for five days and only get paid for three of them? No, he gets paid every time he works. Likewise, every time we are taught the Word, whether it is by the pastor or any other minister, we should be paying them by sowing an offering into their lives.

Someone may be thinking, *I don't believe we should pay for the Gospel!* Do you know what? Neither do I, but I have enough sense to know that even though the Gospel is free, it takes money to get it out to the world! It takes money to build churches, print books, preach on the radio and television, travel overseas and do all the other things required to effectively minister the Word of God to people all over the world.

Some people think that the pastor or traveling minister can just use all the monies that are received during church services for their own personal use, but that simply is not true. They may receive a salary out of those monies, but the rest goes toward the business needs of the ministry. Those needs may be greater or smaller, depending on the size of the particular ministry. Nonetheless, this verse in Galatians tells us that each time we are taught the Word of God it is our responsibility to pay the man or woman of God for their service.

Does this mean that we just put *money* into their hands? No it doesn't. Notice what our verse says: **Let him that is taught in the word communicate unto him that teacheth in all good things.** It says we are to share *in all good things.* That doesn't just mean money. If you see your pastor in need of a home, car, clothing or something else, and you have the means to buy it for him, then do it! If God lays it on your heart to give a minister some jewelry, real estate, stocks or other things besides money, then obey Him. Maybe you have a business where you could sow your services or materials into their lives. I am using just a few examples to expand your thinking about how to sow into the lives of ministers. This verse also says to sow all *good* things. Not some broken down, worn-out thing! Give them your best, and God will give you His!

Then God gives a warning: **Be not deceived; God is not mocked: for whatsoever a man soweth, that shall he also reap.**

Notice, it says, *whatsoever a man sows.* Now, don't take this out of its context. God has just finished telling us that we are supposed to sow to the one who taught us the Word. Then, in essence, He says, "Make no mistakes about it, you can't fool God; you are going to sow something, and whatever you sow is what you are going to reap." That is what He means when He uses the word *whatsoever*. In other words, He is saying that in one way or the other, we are going to sow after we have been taught the Word. Whether we sow to ourselves (by not giving) or sow to the minister (by giving), both are considered sowing in God's eyes! He elaborates further in the next verse: **For he that soweth to his flesh shall of the flesh reap corruption; but he that soweth to the Spirit shall of the Spirit reap life everlasting.**

Can you see it? When we are taught the Word of God and yet don't sow into that minister's life, we are in fact sowing to our own flesh! But that doesn't bring us blessings; on the contrary, it brings corruption to our harvests. The Greek word for *corruption* means "decay, i.e. ruin (spontaneous or inflicted, lit. Or fig.):—corruption, destroy, perish."[2] Well, I don't know about you, but I don't want corruption or decay working in my finances that will ruin an opportunity for financial freedom and cause my blessings to be destroyed and perish right before my eyes!

So how do I avoid that? This verse lets me know that when I give an offering to the minister who has taught me, I am in fact sowing to the Spirit. That means that God will be involved with my harvest! It says, **He that soweth to the Spirit shall of the Spirit reap life everlasting.**

The words *life everlasting* are not referring to our going to heaven when we die. The Greek word for *life* is **zoe.** Vine's explains that this word continually expresses "all of the highest and best which the saints possess in God."[3] In other words, this is talking about the life of God that is in us. The Greek word for *everlasting* means "perpetual,"[4] which simply means it does not cease or end. Therefore, this verse is telling us that when we give a financial or material gift to the minister who has taught us the Word of God, we are actually sowing seeds into God's kingdom. This causes His Spirit to be involved in multiplying the seeds that we have sown, thus perpetually releasing the very life of God into our financial situations. That sounds like something we should want to do continually, and that is why the verse goes on to say, **And let us not be weary in well doing.**

Notice that God says when we give to ministers who feed us the Word, we are *doing well.* And if there is anything you want to hear from God at the end of this life's journey, it is *"Well done,* thou good and faithful servant." I don't believe anyone wants to hear God say, "Well, you're done, servant." No! We want to hear Him say, "Well done!" So God tells us here not to grow weary or tired in our giving. I believe one thing that He means here is that we are not supposed to grow tired of giving every time we are fed. Look at it as an opportunity, not a hardship. Another thing that I believe He is indicating here is that we are not to let our faith grow weak and tired, as that will cause us to faint. We must continue hearing the Word in order to keep our faith from becoming weak and causing us to have what I call "heart failure." What I mean by that is to stop believing. Faith doesn't come from having heard—it comes from continually hearing the Word of God. Therefore, if faith comes by hearing, then faith leaves by not hearing. When we quit hearing the Word of God concerning His laws of increase it will cause us to become weary in well doing. When you become weary you will loosen your grip, and if you stay weary long enough, you will faint, which will cause you to let go of the blessing of God. However, God wants us to keep our faith strong, believing that our harvests are on the way. That is why He said, **For in due season we shall reap, if we faint not.**

This verse doesn't say we might reap, it says we shall reap! But when is *due season?* The Greek word for *due* means "pertaining to self, i.e. one's own."[5] The Greek word for *season* means "an occasion, i.e. set or proper time."[6] In essence, this is telling us that every time we sow we are actually setting our own times for our harvests. It is like the farmer who sows his field; once he sows it, then he has a set time for his own harvest. And as long as he takes care of it and protects it, then that set time will come along and he will enjoy his harvest!

Now think about this: A farmer can only plant and reap harvests at certain times during the year, because he is planting into natural ground; but you and I can plant and reap harvests continually, because we are planting into the supernatural ground of the Spirit! Consequently, in the next verse, God encourages us to take advantage of every opportunity. **As we have therefore opportunity, let us do good unto all men, especially unto them who are of the household of faith.**

When do we have an opportunity to sow for our harvests? Every time our pastors feed us the Word, every time a traveling minister gives us a good meal and every time we go to a special meeting. Furthermore, if you are being fed continually by a certain television or radio preacher, then sow into his or her life too! You will be blessed for it! It is an opportunity to grow in the Word, bless the minister that fed you and sow for your own appointed times of harvest.

✦ ✦ ✦

GOD'S RICHES IN GLORY

*Y*ou have probably heard some Christians say, "My God shall supply all of my needs according to His riches in glory." They were quoting a verse found in Philippians 4:19. It is a wonderful verse of Scripture that gets people excited because they think that if they quote the verse long enough, then God will bring them the resources needed for every situation of lack and deficiency in their lives. However, that may or may not be the case. I have heard people quote this verse who are not qualified for its benefits! Paul is not saying that God will supply all your needs because you are a Christian or because you confess this verse. Let's look closely at the previous verses to see if we can find out how to qualify for God's supplying of our needs from His riches in glory. Philippians 4:15-19 reads:

> Now ye Philippians know also, that in the beginning of the gospel, when I departed from Macedonia, no church communicated with me as concerning giving and receiving, but ye only. For even in Thessalonica ye sent once and again unto my necessity. Not because I desire a gift: but I

desire fruit that may abound to your account. But I have all, and abound: I am full, having received of Epaphroditus the things which were sent from you, an odour of a sweet smell, a sacrifice acceptable, wellpleasing to God. But my God shall supply all your need according to His riches in glory by Christ Jesus.

Paul tells the Philippians that when he started his traveling ministry they were the only church that supported him from Macedonia, and that caused them to come in contact with God's divine law of giving and receiving. He said, **No church communicated with me as concerning giving and receiving, but ye only.**

The word *communicated* means "to (have) come into communion or fellowship with, to become a sharer, be made a partner."[1] This lets us know that they had become partners with him through their giving and that they were sharing in the law of giving and receiving. In other words, when they gave to Paul's ministry they were operating according to the law of seedtime and harvest; therefore, they expected to receive a harvest from their giving. Verse 16 indicates that they supported Paul regularly and didn't grow weary in their well doing: **For even in Thessalonica ye sent once and again unto my necessity.** They kept sending Paul offerings because Paul had a big vision to reach people with the Gospel, and his vision created great needs in his life and ministry. The word *necessity* in this verse doesn't mean that Paul was a poor, needy fellow. In verse 12 he does say that there were times when he had abounded and there were times when he had been in need. Yet in verse 11, he says that he learned to be content in every situation that he faced.

Live Independently of Your Circumstances
♦ ♦ ♦

Unfortunately, some Christians have used these verses to teach that Paul was poor and, therefore, that we, like him, must accept whatever circumstances we find ourselves in, understanding that this is our lot in life and that there is nothing we can do to change it. But this simply isn't true! Look at what Paul said in verse 11: **Not that I speak in respect of want: for I have learned, in whatsoever state I am, therewith to be content.**

The Twentieth Century New Testament says, **For I, however I am placed, have learnt to be independent of my circumstances.** *The New English Bible* says, **I have learned to find resources in myself whatever my circumstances.**

The word *content* comes from two Greek words which basically mean to be "self sufficient."[2] Of course, we know that when Paul said this, he was actually looking to the greater One on the inside of him, because he went on to say, **I can do all things through Christ which strengtheneth me** (v. 13).

So what was Paul saying here? He was saying that he learned to draw his satisfaction and contentment from the Lord and didn't let what was going on around him affect him. Then, in verse 12, he tells us some of what he had been facing in his life, saying,

> **I know both how to be abased, and I know how to abound: every where and in all things I**

am instructed both to be full and to be hungry, both to abound and to suffer need.

In other words, there were times in his life when he was hungry and suffering need, and there were other times when he was full and had plenty. If you read Paul's testimony to the Corinthian church in 2 Corinthians 11:23-27, you can get an even better idea of what he had faced.

In these verses, he says that he had been in prison frequently, near death often, whipped on five occasions, beaten with rods three times, stoned once and shipwrecked three times. Many times he was hungry and thirsty and went without food; and he even had times when he shivered in the cold, not having enough clothing to keep himself warm.

It is very obvious from what he says here that there were surely times when he was suffering need, but he didn't stay there—*and we don't have to either!* Look at what he said to Timothy: **What persecutions I endured: but out of them all the Lord delivered me** (2 Tim. 3:11). In other words, Paul didn't stay abased, in need or in hunger, because God delivered him!

It Is a Win-Win Situation

✦ ✦ ✦

So the Philippian church, knowing Paul's great vision and need, was constantly giving into his life and ministry and operating according to the law of seedtime and harvest. Now look at Philippians 4:17. Paul makes an attention-getting statement that reveals his main motive for desiring their partnership: **Not because I desire a gift: but I desire fruit that may abound to your account.**

In other words, Paul was saying, "I don't want you to give into my life and ministry just because you have seen the needs. My main desire is for you to give so that your heavenly bank account will abound with blessings!" According to verse 18, Paul already had more than enough and was abounding, but that didn't stop him from encouraging them to give, because he knew that they would be blessed financially and materially if they obeyed God's Word by supporting him. Because of their giving, Paul's ministry was flourishing. Notice, Paul said, **But I have all, and abound: I am full, having received of Epaphroditus the things which were sent from you....**

The word *abound* means "to superabound" or "to be in excess."[3] In other words, Paul's life and ministry were being blessed to the point of excess where he had too much money and too many things coming to him. He had too much stuff! Well, isn't that just like God? Isn't He the God who is more than enough, the God of too much? Yes He is, and He hasn't changed; He still wants people to be abundantly provided for today.

If believers *today* would act like the Philippian church, then all the churches, pastors and other ministries would have more than enough finances to do the work God has called them to do. And not only that, but all the believers would have harvests so large that they would be looking for additional places to sow seed!

As far as their offerings were concerned, Paul said in verse 18 that each time they gave it was ...**an odour of a sweet smell, a sacrifice acceptable, wellpleasing to God.** That tells me that they must have given their offerings in faith, because their offerings not only blessed Paul but they pleased God too! When we become partners with good ministers, our gifts, when given in faith, are like a sweet aroma to God. He accepts them as a sacrifice on our part and is thoroughly pleased. Wow! I don't know about you, but that makes me want to give more; and that is exactly what God's Word should do!

My God Shall Supply
✦ ✦ ✦

Now, I hope you have your shoutin' clothes on. If you don't, then go change quickly and then continue reading because this next verse is going to make you want to shout! Paul begins by saying, **But my God shall supply all your need....** Did you notice that Paul said *my God*? Well, wasn't Paul's God the same God the Philippians served? Certainly He was! Then why didn't Paul say, "*Your* God shall supply all your needs"? Because Paul was letting them know that their sowing had caused them to tap into the anointing that God had placed upon his life and ministry, and that anointing was going to bless their finances and destroy yokes of lack and poverty in their lives!

It is important to know what kind of ground you are sowing into. A farmer doesn't just throw his seed on any old ground. He makes sure the ground is good, fertile ground so that it will maximize his harvest. Make sure you do the same. If you are in a good church, one that is teaching you how to walk in victory in all areas of your life, then make sure you are sowing into your pastor's life as well as that of the local church. No, you won't get a tax-deductible receipt when you give to your pastor personally, but I guarantee that you will get a heavenly one. God's payback system is a whole lot better than just a tax deduction! If you are not in a church that is getting people saved, filled with the Holy Ghost, healed, delivered and set free in all areas of their lives, then change churches! Find a good church with a good pastor so you have good ground to sow into.

Then, as you continue to sow into your pastor and church, find other good ministers and ministries to partner with by giving into their personal lives as well as their ministries. Did you notice that I said *good* ministers? How can you tell if they are good ministers? Because when you sit under their ministry and get to know them, you really enjoy being fed by them and you have a sense of being connected with them. When this happens, God is leading you to sow into their ministries.

I believe that this is a part of what Paul was talking about when he said to **know them which labour among you** in 1 Thessalonians 5:12. In fact, verse 13 tells us that after we see them working a good work for God, then we are to esteem them highly. One way of doing that is to be a blessing to them by supporting them with our finances, prayers and time. This will cause our harvests to be even greater because when we water others, then God will see to it that we are watered ourselves. (See Proverbs 11:24-25.)

A Full Supply

✦ ✦ ✦

So, if you, like the church at Philippi, are giving constantly into the lives of anointed men and women of God, then activate your faith by confessing this verse, and receive the benefits that it has to offer. And what are those benefits? Look again at Philippians 4:19: **God shall supply all your need....**

The Greek word used here for *need* is eye opening! Do you remember the phrase, *him that needeth,* that we looked at back in chapter 14? The word *need* used here in Philippians is the same Greek word. Let me refresh your memory on what it means: "employment, i.e. an affair; also (by impl.) occasion, demand, requirement or destitution:—business, lack, necessary, need, use, want."[4] Wow, can you see it? God wants to go way beyond just meeting our needs! He wants to take care of our employment, occasions that might arise, demands placed on us financially, requirements that we may have, our businesses, anything we may lack or need and our wants and desires as well!

Glory to God! What an awesome God we serve. He really is El Shaddai, the God who is more than enough! I am reminded of several other verses that show how He wants to provide for us. Psalm 23:1 says, **The Lord is my shepherd; I shall not want.** Psalm 34:10 reads, **...they that seek the Lord shall not want any good thing.** Notice that God wants to go way beyond just supplying our needs. In fact, if you want something else to shout about, look at the first part of Philippians 4:19 again: **But my God shall supply all your need....** Notice that it says that my God *shall* supply! There are no "if's", "and's", "but's", "might's" or "maybe's" about it! If we do our part, God *will* do His.

Now look at the word *supply*. The Greek word means "to make full, to fill up, i.e. to fill to the full, to cause to abound, to furnish or supply liberally."[5] God doesn't want you to just have enough to get by; He wants to cram the blessings all the way to the top! The word used here is the same word Paul used in the previous verse, where he said, "I am *full*." God wants us to be full in every area.

Also, did you notice that He said that He wants to supply *all* of our need? God wants to cram up to the top and fully supply all of our *employment* needs, provide us with the finances to meet all of the *demands,* or *requirements,* that we may be facing, bless our *businesses* and bring us all of the business that we want, replenish anything that we are *lacking,* take care of all of our *needs*, furnish whatever we may need to *use* and satisfy our every *want* and desire! That is what this verse is really saying.

Unlimited Supply

✦ ✦ ✦

Then God puts the "icing on the cake" at the end of Philippians 4:19. He says that He will provide for us in abundance ...**according to His riches in glory by Christ Jesus.**

When we sow into anointed men and women of God, we tap into a heavenly financial system called *glory!* And *glory* is full of riches and operated by Jesus, the anointed One! When we work within this system, we take off all the limits! It no longer matters what county, state or country we live in, what our age is, what our skin color is, how educated we are, how we were raised, what kind of job we have, how many times we have failed, whether our spouse is saved or how much talent we have or don't have. No! No! No! Thank God this system is based on *His* riches in *glory!*

Never again should you allow the devil to hoodwink you into believing that God just wants to give you enough to get by. And when someone says, "Just hold on 'til the end, Brother, and when you get to the sweet by and by, everything will be okay," you can stand up and say, "I'm not going to hold on until the end. I'm going to go to the end in a blaze of glory, because God is my provider, and He will provide abundantly for me in the sweet here and now!"

CHAPTER 17

✦ ✦ ✦

MAXIMIZING YOUR RETURNS

*H*ave you ever known any Christians who have given large sums of money as offerings and yet never received the bountiful harvest that God has promised? It may be because they don't understand what an important role our mouths play in the giving of our offerings, just as they do in the paying of our tithes. Look again at 2 Corinthians 9:6:

> **But this I say, He which soweth sparingly shall reap also sparingly; and he which soweth bountifully shall reap also bountifully.**

This verse reveals to us that there are two ways to give when we are sowing financial seed and that both ways shall cause a harvest to come. The reaping, or harvesting, will *always* be in direct proportion to *what* we sow and *how* we sow our seed. The first way that is mentioned is to give *sparingly,* and the second way that is mentioned is to give *bountifully.* We learned what giving sparingly is all about back in chapter 13, and found out that we can't be stingy givers if we want a bountiful harvest. Now let's study what it means to give bountifully. The verse says, ...**he which soweth bountifully shall reap also bountifully.**

Look at the word *bountifully* in this verse. By looking at this word in its context and by considering other Scriptures that we have already studied, we can conclude that it must be, at least in part, referring to the size of the gift. However, if bountiful sowing just referred to the size of the gift, then that would mean that everyone who gave a large gift would reap a big harvest; yet we know that doesn't happen. So, there must be more to sowing bountifully than meets the eye.

Actually the Greek word used here is *eulogia,* which means "fine speaking."[1] It comes from the Greek word *eulogeo,* which means "to speak well of, i.e. (religiously) to bless (thank or invoke a benediction upon, prosper)."[2] In other words, we have to speak blessings over our seeds when we give so that they will prosper. If we want to sow bountifully, then we have to get our mouths involved in our giving. Bountiful giving incorporates the mouth just as much as it does the physical act of writing out the check or planting the seed.

We find this same Greek word *eulogia* in James 3:10, which says, **Out of the same mouth proceedeth** *blessing* **and cursing.** James is referring here to believers who only control their tongues part of the time. In essence, he says that in one moment they are speaking fine words, or blessings, out of their mouths; but the next moment they speak curses. Then he says that this should not be happening! Why? Because we are children of the light. We have been translated out of the kingdom of darkness into the kingdom of light. It should be just as foreign for a child of God to utter words out of his mouth that are contrary to God's Word as it is for a freshwater fountain to yield saltwater or an orange tree to grow bananas!

When we say anything contrary to God's Word, we are speaking a curse; and that is tantamount to speaking death over the situation. Do you remember Deuteronomy 30:19? God says, **I have set before you life and death, blessing and cursing: therefore choose life, that both thou and thy seed may live.** Then in Proverbs 18:21, He says, **Death and life are in the power of the tongue.** You could paraphrase it this way: "Blessing and cursing are in the power of the tongue." Only by speaking God's Word can we release the power of life over our giving and then watch the bountiful blessings begin to pour into our lives. This is also how we activate our faith so that our giving will please God.

When Jesus taught his disciples how to use the faith that God gave them, He said that they would have to speak words. (See Mark 11:23-24 and Luke 17:5-6.) That is the way you get the faith that you have in your heart working for you. That faith principle applies in all areas of our lives, including our finances. So, that is why, here in 2 Corinthians 9:6, God uses a word (bountifully) that means we have to speak a blessing over the seeds we sow. We have to speak well of them if we want our faith to work and cause us to reap bountifully.

Back in chapter 13, entitled "The Law of Seedtime and Harvest," we saw that God's system will bring forth fruit when we plant seeds. But verse 29 tells us that we have to *put in the sickle.* I am convinced that this is talking about using our faith. Whether it is a harvest of salvation, healing, prosperity or anything else, we have to release our faith from our hearts *through our mouths.*

I believe that this is where many Christians are missing it concerning their financial harvests. They plant good seed in good ground, but then they are saying things like "We just never have enough," or "We can't afford that," or "Every time we get a little extra saved up, something happens and we have to spend it all." God has the answer: **...for out of the abundance of the heart, the mouth speaketh** (Matt. 12:34). People have allowed themselves to be swayed by everything from newspapers to television broadcasts and even by what their poverty-minded Uncle Henry said! They have filled their hearts with a bunch of doubt and unbelief. Therefore, they expect the worst and then release curses out of their mouths by speaking out the doubt and unbelief.

Unfortunately, this has even caused many of them to start "saving up for a rainy day." Listen, if that is what you are doing, then sooner or later the devil will rain on your parade! You need to plan for your savings being used for enjoying life; and then, instead of saving up for a rainy day, you will start *sowing for a harvest today!* At least that way if a rainy day does come, you will know that your supply won't get depleted, because God and His riches in glory are your source, not your money. In fact, that kind of thinking and talking will eventually get you to the place where you will have so much left over that you will be able to help someone else out of his rainy day!

So, giving bountifully means to give continually and in greater amounts; but, just as importantly, it also means to speak words over your offerings that are in line with the Word of God. Bountiful giving incorporates the heart and mouth as well as the hand and wallet. Say something like this every time you give into the kingdom of God: "Seed, I am sowing you into the kingdom of God. You go bless this ministry (name the ministry, or the man or woman of God to whom you are sowing) and be multiplied to them, and then bring me back a harvest. And I want it good measure, pressed down, shaken together and running over. Holy Spirit, I expect you to influence men to give into my life. Angels, go forth and cause favor, money and blessings to come my way. I am sowing bountifully; and, therefore, I shall reap bountifully. God is making His grace abound toward me in the area of finances, to the point that all of my needs, wants and desires are met and I have plenty left over to give in excess to every good work of the Gospel!"

Amen, and so be it! From this time forward, let's all be determined to be bountiful givers.

Conclusion

*U*nlike the world's system of prosperity, God's system won't bring sorrow to you but will fill your years with pleasures. God said in Proverbs 10:22, **The blessing of the Lord, it maketh rich, and he addeth no sorrow with it.** The *New International Version* reads, **The blessing of the Lord brings wealth, and he adds no trouble to it.**

God's system of prosperity is absolutely awesome! It is truly no respecter of persons and excludes no one! It doesn't have anything to do with your age, intelligence, nationality, marital status, profession or anything else, because God's system of financial freedom works for everyone who carefully abides by its rules. It doesn't matter if you are a single mother, a retiree, a welfare recipient or an uneducated person. It doesn't matter if you were born on the wrong side of the tracks or raised in a dysfunctional home. It doesn't matter what kind of job you have or don't have. It doesn't depend on your skin color, and it doesn't depend on where you live. It doesn't matter how old or how young you are.

And besides all of that, the returns are phenomenal! All we have to do is what God says to do in His Word.

As we accurately and carefully tithe and give offerings and make them a regular part of our lives, we will open up tremendous opportunities for God to move in our lives and in our finances. In these last days, God is looking for modern-day Abrahams—men and women of God who can handle great amounts of wealth and still be called the friends of God.

Wealth and riches have always been a part of the glory of God; we just didn't know it, and therefore couldn't partake of it. But God said in Haggai that He is pouring out His glory in these last days greater than ever before. And the silver and the gold are part of His glory. So what are you waiting for? Put God first in your life, seek His ways and live by His system of prosperity, then stand back and see what He will do.

> I will fill this house with glory, saith the Lord of hosts. The silver is mine, and the gold is mine, saith the Lord of hosts. The glory of this latter house shall be greater than of the former, saith the Lord of hosts: and in this place will I give peace.
>
> —HAGGAI 2:7-9

ENDNOTES

Chapter 1
[1]Vine, p. 685.
[2]Strong, "Greek," #932.
[3]Strong, "Greek," #1849.
[4]Strong, "Greek," #1391.
[5]Strong, "Greek," #3860.

Chapter 3
[1]Strong, "Greek," #61.
[2]Unger, p. 54.
[3]Strong, "Greek," #5224.

Chapter 4
[1]Strong, "Greek," #4052.
[2]*Enhanced Strong's Lexicon.*
[3]Ibid.
[4]Ibid.
[5]Strong, "Greek," #4147.

Chapter 5
[1]Strong, "Greek," #2730.
[2]Strong, "Greek," #3614.

Chapter 6
[1]Strong, "Greek," #2172.
[2]Strong, "Greek," #2137.
[3]Strong, "Greek," #5198.
[4]Vine, P. 588.
[5]*Enhanced Strong's Lexicon.*

Chapter 8
[1]Strong, "Greek," #841.
[2]Strong, "Greek," #4200.
[3]Strong, "Greek," #3173.
[4]Strong, "Greek," #3713.
[5]Strong, "Greek," #4124.
[6]Strong, "Greek," #4146.
[7]Vine, p. 533.
[8]Strong, "Greek," #5309.
[9]Strong, "Greek," #1679.

Chapter 9
[1]Vine, p. 219.
[2]Strong, "Hebrew," #623.

Chapter 10
[1]Strong, "Hebrew," #618.
[2]Strong, "Hebrew," #7647.
[3]Strong, "Hebrew," #1952.
[4]Strong, "Hebrew," #7225.
[5]Strong, "Hebrew," #8393.
[6]*Enhanced Strong's Lexicon.*
[7]Ibid.
[8]Strong, "Greek," #5303.
[9]Walvoord, p. 256.

Chapter 11
[1]Strong, "Hebrew," #398.

Chapter 12
[1]Strong, "Greek," #1577.
[2]Strong, "Hebrew," #935.

[3]Strong, "Hebrew," #974.
[4]Strong, "Hebrew," #699.
[5]Strong, "Hebrew," #1605.

Chapter 13
[1]Strong, "Greek," #4255.
[2]Strong, "Greek," #4052.
[3]Strong, "Greek," #5340.
[4]*God's Word to the Nations.*

Chapter 14
[1]Strong, "Greek," #2872.
[2]Strong, "Greek," #2038.
[3]Strong, "Greek," #5532.
[4]Strong, "Greek," #2040, 2041.
[5]Strong, "Greek," #3408.
[6]Strong, "Greek," #4291.
[7]Strong, "Greek," #2573.
[8]Vine, p. 207.
[9]*Enhanced Strong's Lexicon.*
[10]Strong, "Greek," #5092.
[11]*Enhanced Strong's Lexicon.*
[12]Strong, "Greek," #80.

Chapter 15
[1]*Enhanced Strong's Lexicon.*
[2]Strong, "Greek," #5356.
[3]Vine, p. 37.
[4]Strong, "Greek," #166.
[5]Strong, "Greek," #2398.
[6]Strong, "Greek," #2540.

Chapter 16

[1]*Enhanced Strong's Lexicon.*
[2]Vine, p. 125.
[3]Stong, "Greek," #4052.
[4]Strong, "Greek," #5532.
[5]*Enhanced Strong's Lexicon.*

Chapter 17

[1]Strong, "Greek," #2129.
[2]Strong, "Greek," #2127.

REFERENCES

Enhanced Strong's Lexicon. Oak Harbor, WA: Logos Research System, Inc., 1995.

God's Word to the Nations. Grand Rapids, MI: World Publishing, 1997.

Strong, James. *Strong's Exhaustive Concordance of the Bible.* "Hebrew and Chaldee Dictionary," "Greek Dictionary of the New Testament." Nashville: Abingdon, 1890.

Unger, Merrill F. *Unger's Bible Dictionary.* Chicago: Moody Press, 1966.

Vine, W.E., Merrill F. Unger and William White, Jr., *An Expository Dictionary of Biblical Words.* Nashville: Thomas Nelson, 1985.

Walvoord, John F. and Roy B. Zuck. *The Bible Knowledge Commentary.* Wheaton, IL: Scripture Press Publications, 1983, 1985.

BIBLIOGRAPHY

ABOUT THE AUTHOR

LARRY HUTTON is a dynamic teacher and preacher for the body of Christ today! He teaches and preaches with a prophetic voice that is changing the lives of multitudes.

In 1980, God spoke to Larry in an audible voice and said, "Keep it simple. My Word is simple!" With that mandate from heaven, Larry has become widely acclaimed for the clarity and simplicity with which he teaches God's Word. He believes that the Bible is for us today and that we ought to be able to understand what it is saying so we can apply it and reach our God-given potential. He also believes that we don't have to wait until we get to the "sweet by and by" before we can enjoy God's blessings, but that God wants us to enjoy them in the "sweet here and now!"

Larry is nationally known as a speaker, singer and author, and has become a popular guest speaker at church meetings, seminars, campmeetings and on Christian television. His teachings on divine healing, prosperity and victorious Christian living have challenged and helped many ministers and laymen alike around the world to strive for God's best in their lives.

While his ministry produces a wide variety of audio and video teaching tapes, Larry is perhaps best known for his unique and extremely popular series of Scripture tapes, "Heaven's Health Food," "Heaven's Wealth Food" and "Power Up!" Each tape features Larry speaking multiple translations of many verses applicable to the title subject, thereby bringing incredible clarity to the Word. Presented over a soft instrumental background, these tapes lend themselves to repeated listening. As a result, thousands of people have been healed, encouraged and set free by "hearing and hearing" the Word of God as presented on these tapes. LARRY HUTTON MINISTRIES also publishes and distributes a free periodical called THE FORCE OF FAITH. Read by many thousands of people, its articles are educational, uplifting, inspiring and encouraging.

Larry and his wife, Liz, travel extensively and also conduct regularly scheduled meetings at the LARRY HUTTON MINISTRIES headquarters in Broken Arrow, Oklahoma.

VERY IMPORTANT MESSAGE

God wants a personal relationship with every person in the world, including you! God is not mad at you, and He is not counting up all of your sins and holding them against you. He sent Jesus Christ to shed His blood and then be raised from the dead, just so that you can be freed from the bondage of sin and enter into eternal life with a loving heavenly Father.

If you've never accepted Jesus Christ as your personal Lord and Savior, it's very simple. The Bible states in Romans 10:13, **Whosoever calls on the name of the Lord shall be saved.** Since it says **whosoever**, then your name is in the Bible! In verses 9 and 10 we're told how easy it is to become saved. It tells us that if we say with our mouths that Jesus is our Lord, and we believe with our hearts that God raised Him from the dead, we ...**shall be saved.** It's that easy!

If you've never done this, then do it today! Say this prayer out loud right now:

Dear God, I want to be part of Your family. You said that if I would confess Jesus as the Lord of my life and believe in my heart that You raised Him from the dead, I would be saved. So, God, I now say that Jesus is the Lord of my life. I believe in my heart that You raised Him from the dead and that He lives forevermore. I accept my salvation now in the name of Jesus. Thank You, God, for forgiving me, saving me and giving me eternal life. Amen!

If you just prayed this prayer for the first time, I welcome you to the family of God! Now it is very important, as a newborn child of God, that you get fed the milk of God's holy Word so that you can grow up in God.

Please write, fax or e-mail us at the addresses below so we can send you some free literature to help you in your new walk with the Lord. If you wish, we will also try to help you find a good church home.

LARRY HUTTON MINISTRIES
P.O. BOX 822
BROKEN ARROW, OKLAHOMA 74013-0822
(918) 259-3158 (fax) admin@lhm.net (e-mail)

To contact Larry Hutton,
write:

Larry Hutton
P.O. Box 822
Broken Arrow, Oklahoma 74013-0822

Or use one of the following methods:
(918) 259-3158 (fax) admin@lhm.net (e-mail)

*Please include your prayer requests
and comments when you write.*

Additional copies of this book
are available from your local bookstore.

HARRISON HOUSE
Tulsa, Oklahoma 74153

THE HARRISON HOUSE VISION

Proclaiming the truth and the power
Of the Gospel of Jesus Christ
With excellence;
Challenging Christians to
Live victoriously,
Grow spiritually,
Know God intimately.